# *breakfast*
## & BRUNCH ™

# 60

CHIPOTLE BACON
BREAKFAST
SANDWICHES

**VARIETY-PACK DONUT
MUFFINS, PAGE 20**

# CONTENTS

This book is brought to you by the editors of **CUISINE**® AT HOME Magazine. To subscribe, visit **www.cuisineathome.com**

**ISBN#9798628810620**
*Cuisine at Home* Breakfast & Brunch
is published by Active Interest Media
2143 Grand Ave., Des Moines, IA 50312

*Cuisine at Home* is a registered trademark
of Cruz Bay Publishing, Inc.

PRINTED IN THE USA

74

DENVER
OMELET
NACHOS

# FROM THE
# BAKERY

Start your morning on a sweet note with one of these freshly baked treats most certain to make your day.

Brie & Cherry Braid, 6

Cinnamon Roll Coffee Cake with Caramel Topping, 8

New York Crumb Cake, 10

Mocha Coffee Cakes with Chocolate Streusel, 11

Cinnamon Rolls with Vanilla Bean Frosting, 12

Sticky Rolls with Toasted Pecans, 15

Sour Cream Old-Fashioned Doughnuts, 16

Chocolate Old-Fashioned Doughnuts, 19

Variety-Pack Donut Muffins, 20

Cranberry-Pecan Scones with Spiced Orange Marmalade, 22

Basic Buttermilk Biscuits, 24

Apricot Pecan Butter, 25

# Braided Coffee Cake

Creatively flavored and visually impressive, this tart cherry and creamy Brie-filled yeasted coffee cake is a sweet way to start your day. A quick glaze drizzled over the top finishes it off just right. Set it out on the buffet table and you're sure to hear lots of oohs and aahs.

**GOOD TO KNOW:**
Vanilla Bean Paste

Vanilla bean paste is made by infusing vanilla beans into a mixture of sugar, water, vanilla extract, and a thickener for a product that contains visible vanilla bean seeds.

# Brie & Cherry Braid

*Each brand refers to instant-dry yeast differently. You may find it labeled Quick-Rise, RapidRise, Perfect Rise, or bread machine yeast.*

Makes 12 servings
Total time: 1½ hours + rising

**FOR THE DOUGH, HEAT:**
¾   cup whole milk
½   cup granulated sugar
½   tsp. table salt

**COMBINE:**
2½   cups all-purpose flour
1   Tbsp. instant-dry yeast

**ADD:**
1   egg, beaten
1   egg yolk, beaten
4   Tbsp. unsalted butter, cubed and softened

**FOR THE FILLING, PULSE:**
¼   cup dried tart cherries
8   oz. frozen tart cherries, thawed (about 2 cups)
½   cup granulated sugar
4   tsp. cornstarch
1   tsp. vanilla bean paste
8   oz. Brie, rind removed from edge, sliced ¼-inch thick

**BRUSH:**
1   egg, beaten with 1 Tbsp. water
2   Tbsp. sliced almonds

**FOR THE GLAZE, WHISK:**
½   cup powdered sugar, sifted
1   Tbsp. whole milk

**For the dough, heat** milk, granulated sugar, and salt in a saucepan over medium until the sugar dissolves, 1–2 minutes; cool to 100°. Coat a bowl with nonstick spray.

**Combine** flour and yeast in the bowl of a stand mixer fitted with the paddle attachment.

**Add** egg, egg yolk, and milk mixture; blend on medium-low speed until a dough forms. Switch to the dough hook and knead dough until it springs back when pressed with a greased fingertip, 4–5 minutes; scrape down sides and bottom of bowl.

**Add** butter 1 Tbsp. at a time, mixing until incorporated before adding the next, 1–2 minutes. Scrape bottom and sides of the bowl between each addition. Transfer the dough to prepared bowl, cover with plastic wrap, and let rise in a warm place until doubled in size, about 2 hours. Chill the dough overnight.

**For the filling, pulse** dried cherries in a food processor until minced. Add thawed cherries and pulse until nearly minced. Transfer the mixture to a saucepan.

**Whisk** together cherry mixture, granulated sugar, cornstarch, and vanilla bean paste over medium heat until simmering, then cook until thickened, 1 minute; remove from heat and chill in pan until cold.

**Roll** dough on lightly floured parchment paper into a 12×16-inch rectangle. Cut ½-inch-wide strips on outer thirds of dough at a 45-degree angle.

**Lay** Brie slices down center of dough, leaving 2-inch flaps at top and bottom bare; top Brie with cherry mixture. Fold up both end flaps, then braid strips over filling. Slide braid and parchment onto the back of a baking sheet. Cover braid with a towel and let rise until puffy, about 2 hours.

**Preheat** oven to 350°.

**Brush** egg wash over braid. Sprinkle almonds over top and bake braid until golden, about 30 minutes.

**For the glaze, whisk** together powdered sugar and milk. Let braid cool 10 minutes, then drizzle glaze over top. Let braid cool 30 minutes more, then serve.

Per serving: 297 cal; 11g total fat (6g sat); 69mg chol; 234mg sodium; 43g carb; 2g fiber; 9g protein

Cut outer thirds of dough into ½-inch-wide strips so they're a similar size and form a nice braid.

Fold flaps on both ends of the braid up and over the filling. Tuck in the excess dough like bed sheets.

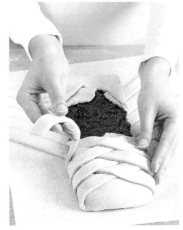

Braid dough strips over the filling by alternating strips from each side. It's OK if some of the fruit leaks out.

# Cinnamon Roll Cake

When it comes to favorite morning pastries to wake up to, many people would likely find it difficult to choose between coffee cake and cinnamon rolls. This breakfast treat combines the best of both worlds into one amazing brunch-worthy baked good.

**TEST KITCHEN TIP:**
**Equipment Note**

A deep cake pan is a must for this cake — the batter fills a 2-inch pan to the rim. To be sure it doesn't overflow, place the filled pan on a foil-lined baking sheet to bake it.

# Cinnamon Roll Coffee Cake
## with caramel topping

*The Test Kitchen prefers pecans in this cake, but feel free to substitute your favorite nut. And vanilla yogurt boosts the flavor, but plain yogurt works, too.*

Makes 10 servings (one 9-inch cake)
Total time: about 1¹/₂ hours

### FOR THE CARAMEL, STIR:
- ³/₄ cup packed brown sugar
- ¹/₄ cup heavy cream
- Pinch of table salt
- 1 cup chopped pecans, toasted

### FOR THE STREUSEL, PULSE:
- ¹/₂ cup packed brown sugar
- ¹/₃ cup all-purpose flour
- 4 Tbsp. unsalted butter, cubed
- 1 Tbsp. ground cinnamon
- ¹/₄ tsp. table salt

### FOR THE CAKE, WHISK:
- 1¹/₂ cups all-purpose flour
- ¹/₂ tsp. *each* baking powder, baking soda, and table salt
- ¹/₂ cup buttermilk
- ¹/₄ cup vanilla yogurt
- 2 eggs
- 1 stick unsalted butter, softened (8 Tbsp.)
- ³/₄ cup granulated sugar

**Preheat** oven to 350°. Coat a 9×2-inch round cake pan with nonstick spray.

**For the caramel, stir** together brown sugar, cream, and pinch of salt. Pour caramel into prepared pan, spreading to coat bottom. Sprinkle pecans over caramel.

**For the streusel, pulse** brown sugar, flour, butter, cinnamon, and salt in a food processor until fine.

**For the cake, whisk** together flour, baking powder, baking soda, and salt.

**Whisk** together buttermilk, yogurt, and eggs in a measuring cup with a pour spout.

**Beat** butter and granulated sugar in a large bowl with a hand mixer just until combined. Alternately add flour mixture and buttermilk mixture to the butter mixture, starting and ending with the flour mixture; blend only enough to incorporate the dry ingredients into the batter.

**Spread** half the batter over the pecans, then sprinkle with half the streusel. Carefully spread remaining batter over streusel; top with remaining streusel.

**Bake** coffee cake until a toothpick inserted in the center comes out clean, 50–60 minutes. Let cake cool 5 minutes on a rack, then run a paring knife around the sides to loosen cake. Invert cake onto a serving plate while hot. Let coffee cake cool slightly before serving.

Per serving: 457 cal; 25g total fat (11g sat); 83mg chol; 306mg sodium; 58g carb; 2g fiber; 5g protein

So the cake unmolds easily, coat the pan well with nonstick spray before adding the caramel and nuts.

To prevent the caramel and nuts from mixing, drop the batter by spoonfuls, then gently spread it.

Sprinkle the streusel mixture evenly over the batter, reserving half of it to sprinkle over the top.

FROM THE
**BAKERY**

# New York Crumb Cake

*This cake may be called New York Crumb Cake but it's based on a European cake brought to the big city by German immigrants in the 1880s.*

Makes 9 servings
Total time: about 1½ hours + cooling

### FOR THE CRUMB TOPPING, COMBINE:

- ½   cup packed light brown sugar
- ¼   cup granulated sugar
- 2½  tsp. ground cinnamon
- ½   tsp. kosher salt
- 1    stick unsalted butter (8 Tbsp.), melted and slightly cooled
- 1½  cups all-purpose flour

### FOR THE CAKE, WHISK:

- 1¼  cups all-purpose flour
- 1    tsp. baking powder
- ½   tsp. kosher salt
- ¼   tsp. baking soda

### CREAM:

- 6    Tbsp. unsalted butter, softened
- 1    cup granulated sugar
- 2    eggs
- 1    tsp. pure vanilla extract
- ½   cup sour cream
       Powdered sugar

**Preheat** oven to 325° with rack in center position. Coat an 8×8-inch baking dish with butter and flour.

**For the crumb topping, combine** brown sugar, granulated sugar, cinnamon, and salt; stir in melted butter, then stir in flour until mixture forms moist clumps.

**For the cake, whisk** together flour, baking powder, salt, and baking soda in a bowl.

**Cream** softened butter and granulated sugar in a separate bowl with a hand mixer on medium-high speed until light and fluffy, 3–5 minutes. Beat in eggs, one at a time, then vanilla, beating just until incorporated. Add sour cream and beat just until blended.

**Beat** in flour mixture in three additions on low speed just until incorporated.

**Transfer** batter to prepared dish; smooth top. Starting at the edges, drop marble-sized pieces of topping evenly over batter. Completely cover cake with crumbs (topping will be thick).

**Bake** cake until topping is golden brown and a toothpick inserted into center of cake comes out clean, 45–50 minutes. Let cake cool completely; sprinkle with powdered sugar before serving.

Per serving: 504 cal; 21g total fat (13g sat); 98mg chol; 336mg sodium; 74g carb; 1g fiber; 6g protein

**To keep from weighing down the center of the cake, evenly arrange the crumbs from the edges inward.**

# Mocha Coffee Cakes
## with chocolate streusel

*With coffee and chocolate, these cakes are a real pick-me-up. For one cake, bake in a greased 10-inch tube (angel food) pan, 50–60 minutes.*

Makes 18 servings
Total time: about 1 hour

**FOR THE TOPPING, COMBINE:**

| | |
|---|---|
| 1/4 | cup chocolate-covered espresso beans, chopped |
| 1/4 | cup mini semisweet chocolate chips |

**FOR THE FILLING, PULSE:**

| | |
|---|---|
| 1/4 | cup sugar |
| 1/4 | cup chocolate-covered espresso beans |
| 3 | Tbsp. unsweetened cocoa powder |
| 4 | oz. bittersweet bar chocolate, chopped |

**FOR THE CAKE, WHISK:**

| | |
|---|---|
| 3 | cups all-purpose flour, sifted |
| 1 1/2 | tsp. baking powder |
| 1 | tsp. table salt |
| 1/2 | tsp. baking soda |

**BEAT:**

| | |
|---|---|
| 2 | sticks unsalted butter (16 Tbsp.), softened |
| 1 | tsp. pure vanilla extract |
| 1 2/3 | cups sugar |
| 3 | eggs |

**STIR:**

| | |
|---|---|
| 1/2 | cup strongly brewed coffee |
| 1 | Tbsp. instant espresso powder |
| 1 1/2 | cups buttermilk |

**Preheat** oven to 350°. Coat three 6-cup popover or muffin pans with nonstick spray.

**For the topping, combine** chopped espresso beans and chocolate chips.

**For the filling, pulse** sugar, espresso beans, cocoa, and chopped chocolate in a food processor until sandy.

**For the cake, whisk** together flour, baking powder, salt, and baking soda in a bowl.

**Beat** butter and vanilla in a bowl with a mixer until smooth.

**With mixer running, gradually beat in** sugar until light and fluffy and all sugar dissolves, about 5 minutes. Beat in eggs.

**Stir** together brewed coffee and espresso powder, then stir into buttermilk. Alternately mix flour mixture and buttermilk mixture into creamed mixture (starting and ending with flour) just to combine.

**Scoop** batter with a #30 scoop (2 Tbsp.) into each prepared cup. Top batter with 1 heaping tsp. filling and a second scoop of batter. Combine remaining filling with topping and sprinkle on cakes. Bake cakes until a toothpick inserted into centers comes out clean, 17–20 minutes. Let cakes cool in pans, 30 minutes, then loosen edges and remove.

Per serving: 332 cal; 16g total fat (10g sat); 60mg chol; 244mg sodium; 45g carb; 1g fiber; 5g protein

To form the marbled layer, simply sprinkle the sandy filling onto the first scoop of batter in the pans.

# SENSATIONAL
# CINNAMON ROLLS

**The aroma of cinnamon rolls baking in the oven** is a guaranteed way to get stragglers out of bed — no one wants to miss out on a warm cinnamon roll.

Besides their wonderful scent, this recipe stands out for its versatility. One dough recipe can be used to make two different types of rolls. Use it to make a classic cinnamon roll with vanilla bean frosting, or a sticky roll with gooey caramel and pecans. It'll be tough deciding which one to make first.

The addition of rolled oats in the dough adds an earthy, nutty flavor. And using shortening in the dough, instead of butter, keeps the rolls super tender, and they'll stay softer longer, that is if they don't all get eaten right away.

## Cinnamon Rolls
### with vanilla bean frosting

*Proof the yeast in the warm milk mixture — it should be foamy and bubbly after 5 minutes. If it's not, check the expiration date on the package of yeast.*

Makes 12 servings; Total time: 1 hour + rising and baking

**FOR THE DOUGH, HEAT:**
1 1/4 cups whole milk
1/2 cup shortening
1/4 cup packed brown sugar
1 pkg. active dry yeast (2 1/4 tsp.)

**SOAK:**
1 cup old-fashioned rolled oats
1/2 cup hot water

**ADD:**
4 cups all-purpose flour
2 eggs
1 1/2 tsp. table salt

**FOR THE FILLING, COMBINE:**
1 1/2 sticks unsalted butter, softened (12 Tbsp.)
1 cup packed brown sugar
2 Tbsp. ground cinnamon
1 tsp. table salt

**FOR THE FROSTING, BEAT:**
4 Tbsp. unsalted butter, softened
8 oz. powdered sugar (2 cups)
2 Tbsp. whole milk
1 1/2 tsp. vanilla bean paste
1/4 tsp. table salt

**For the dough, heat** milk, shortening, and brown sugar in a small saucepan over medium-low until shortening is melted; transfer to the bowl of a stand mixer. Let mixture cool to 100–110°, then whisk in yeast and proof until foamy, about 5 minutes.

**Soak** oats in hot water until all water is absorbed.

**Add** 2 cups flour and eggs to the yeast mixture and mix on low with the paddle attachment until combined. Switch to the dough hook and add remaining 2 cups flour, oats, and salt. Mix on low speed until incorporated, then increase speed to medium and mix until dough pulls away from the side of the bowl, about 7 minutes.

**Transfer** dough to a bowl coated with nonstick spray, cover with plastic wrap, and let rise in a warm place until dough doubles in size, about 2 hours. Lift edges of dough away from bowl and press air bubbles out with your hands.

**For the filling, combine** butter, brown sugar, cinnamon, and salt.

**Coat** a 9×13-inch baking pan with butter. Transfer dough to a floured surface and gently press to remove air bubbles. Divide dough into two pieces and roll one piece into a 10×16-inch rectangle.

**Spread** half the filling over dough, leaving a 1/2-inch border. Starting at the short end, roll dough, jelly roll-style, into a log. Repeat filling and rolling with remaining dough half. Freeze logs 10 minutes to firm.

**Slice** each log into six rolls and arrange in prepared pan. Cover rolls with a towel and let rise until puffy, about 1 hour; remove towel.

**Preheat** oven to 375°.

**For the frosting, beat** butter, powdered sugar, milk, vanilla bean paste, and salt with a mixer until combined.

**Bake** rolls until browned, 30–35 minutes. Cool rolls in the pan for 10 minutes, then top with frosting.

Per serving: 548 cal; 25g total fat (12g sat); 74mg chol; 559mg sodium; 76g carb; 2g fiber; 7g protein

**Once the dough has doubled in size,** it's ready to roll out. Assembling the rolls is simple. Halve the dough, roll out each half, and spread on the filling. When rolling the dough, pull back on it slightly so you get the tightest log — it'll make the rolls easier to cut and handle.

Next is placing the rolls in the pan. For the best presentation when making the Cinnamon Rolls, place the end pieces widest side up.

Mix the dough with the paddle attachment to be sure the eggs get thoroughly incorporated.

Dough should spring back when pressed with a fingertip after kneading with the dough hook.

Lift the edge of the doubled dough and press out the air bubbles to redistribute the yeast cells.

Roll up the dough jelly roll-style, starting on the short side. Freeze logs briefly for easier cutting.

Trim off the ends of the logs with dental floss and discard, then cut each log into six equal pieces.

Arrange the rolls in the prepared pan, presentation side up. Space them equally to allow for rising.

# Pecan Sticky Rolls

If we had to pick a favorite sweet roll in the Test Kitchen, this would be it. The caramel sauce makes these rolls too sticky and gooey to resist. And have patience when turning these babies out of the pan — they need to rest 5 minutes before serving them.

## Sticky Rolls
### with toasted pecans

Makes 12 servings
Total time: 1 hour + rising and baking

**FOR THE CARAMEL, BOIL:**

| | |
|---|---|
| 3/4 | cup packed brown sugar |
| 1/4 | cup heavy cream |
| 2 | Tbsp. light corn syrup |
| 1/2 | tsp. table salt |
| 1 | cup chopped pecans, toasted |

**FOR THE ROLLS, PREPARE:**

1 recipe Cinnamon Rolls, through Step 5 (*pages 13 & 14*)

Pour caramel into pan and allow it to cool down and set up before arranging rolls over the top.

Place the serving platter over the baked rolls, then flip them over and pull the pan off the rolls.

**Coat** a 9×13-inch baking pan with butter; set aside.

**For the caramel, boil** brown sugar, cream, corn syrup, and salt in a saucepan over medium-low heat, 2 minutes. Pour caramel into prepared pan, then sprinkle pecans over caramel; cool.

**For the rolls, prepare** one recipe Cinnamon Rolls.

**Preheat** oven to 375°.

**Arrange** rolls on top of caramel. Cover with a towel and let rise until puffy, about 1 hour; remove towel.

**Bake** rolls until browned, 30–35 minutes. Let rolls rest 5 minutes in the pan, then turn out onto a serving platter.

Per serving: 597 cal; 30g total fat (12g sat); 71mg chol; 622mg sodium; 77g carb; 3g fiber; 8g protein

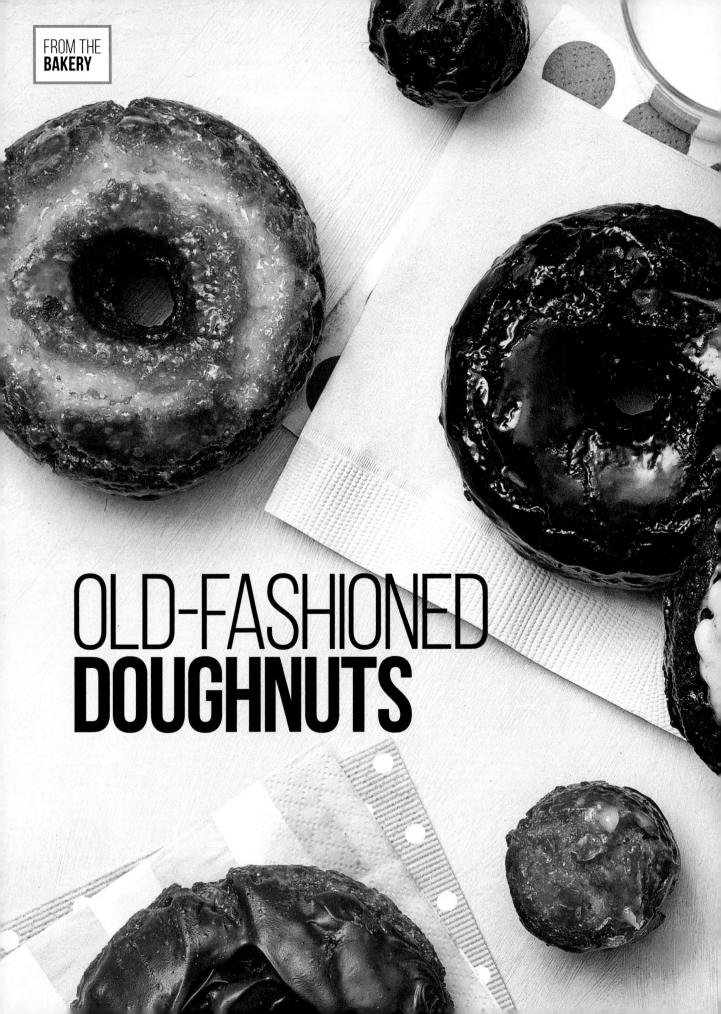

# OLD-FASHIONED
# DOUGHNUTS

**Old-fashioned doughnuts are a rare treat,** and once you take a bite into one of these fresh ones, you may never be able to eat store-bought doughnuts again. And because old-fashioned doughnuts are fried at a lower temperature than regular cake doughnuts, or their fluffy yeast cousins, their tops crack, resulting in doughnuts with crunchy outsides and soft, cakey insides.

Making these doughnuts with sour cream and cake flour keeps them tender, while mace brings some warmth. And if you're a chocolate fan, we've got you covered — with the glaze and icing, too.

After frying, dip the hot doughnuts in the glaze — this keeps them fresher longer. Of course, icing is here too, and is just as good. And lastly, be sure to fry the doughnut holes — kids love them!

## Sour Cream Old-Fashioned Doughnuts

*Because this dough can chill overnight, all you have to do in the morning is roll it out, cut the doughnuts, fry, and glaze them.*

Makes 10 servings
(10 doughnuts + holes)
Total time: 1½ hours + chilling

**WHISK:**

| | |
|---|---|
| 3¾ | cups cake flour |
| 4 | tsp. baking powder |
| 1 | Tbsp. ground mace |
| 1½ | tsp. table salt |

**BEAT:**

| | |
|---|---|
| 1 | cup granulated sugar |
| 4 | Tbsp. cold shortening, cubed |
| 3 | egg yolks |
| 1¼ | cups sour cream |
| | Peanut oil |

**Whisk** together flour, baking powder, mace, and salt.

**Beat** sugar and shortening in the bowl of a stand mixer with the paddle attachment until thoroughly combined. Add yolks and beat until pale in color. Add sour cream and beat to combine. With the mixer on low, add flour mixture little by little until all is added and dough is combined.

**Wrap** dough in plastic and chill 1 hour or up to overnight.

**Prepare** glaze according to directions, *page 18*. Heat 2-inches oil in a large high-sided cast-iron skillet or pot to 340°.

**Roll** dough on a floured surface to ½–¾-inch thick. Cut doughnuts using a 3¼-inch round cutter. Cut holes with a 1¼-inch round cutter. Reroll scraps once. Brush excess flour from doughnuts.

**Fry** doughnuts in hot oil, in batches of two or three, 45 seconds, then flip and fry 1½ minutes; flip again and fry 45 seconds more. Transfer doughnuts using a slotted spoon to a wire rack set inside a baking sheet. When cool enough to handle, but still hot, dip cracked side of doughnuts in glaze; shake off excess and return to rack. Once glaze is slightly set, dip doughnuts again on same side. Allow glaze to set completely, 15 minutes.

**If using icing, dip** the cracked side of the doughnuts in glaze once and let cool completely, then dip glazed side in icing. Let icing set before serving.

Per serving double-dipped in vanilla glaze: 753 cal; 26g total fat (8g sat); 75mg chol; 632mg sodium; 128g carb; 1g fiber; 6g protein

Mace is the red lacy membrane covering a nutmeg seed. It has a similar, but more pungent, flavor.

Adding the flour little by little allows it to be blended in without overmixing the dough.

Bloom cocoa in hot water to bring out its flavor and get rid of the raw, dusty quality it can have.

For smooth glazes and icings, sift powdered sugar and cocoa to get rid of any lumps.

Dipping doughnuts in glaze while they're warm leaves a nice, thin coating and seals in freshness.

Icings should be loose enough to dip tops of doughnuts, but not so loose they run like the glazes.

**Glazes & Icings**: Both glazes and icings should be made just before using. Apply glazes to hot doughnuts but icings to cool ones. If either thickens too much, add hot water, a teaspoon at a time, to thin them. Each glaze recipe makes enough to double-dip one recipe of doughnuts and holes. Each icing recipe makes enough to single-dip one recipe of doughnuts and holes.

**Vanilla Glaze:** Sift 6 cups powdered sugar. Add 3/4 cup hot water, 1/4 cup light corn syrup, 2 tsp. vanilla bean paste, and 1/4 tsp. table salt; whisk until smooth. Cover glaze with plastic wrap while frying doughnuts.

**Chocolate Glaze:** Sift 1/4 cup unsweetened cocoa powder; whisk in 3/4 cup hot water until cocoa dissolves. Sift 6 cups powdered sugar. Add cocoa mixture, 1/4 cup light corn syrup, and 1/4 tsp. table salt; whisk until smooth. Cover glaze with plastic wrap while frying doughnuts.

**Vanilla Icing:** Sift 3 cups powdered sugar and beat with 1/4 cup hot water, 1 tsp. light corn syrup, 1 tsp. vanilla bean paste, and 1/4 tsp. table salt with a mixer until combined. Ice doughnuts immediately after making icing.

**Chocolate Icing:** Sift 3 cups powdered sugar and beat with 1/2 cup hot water, 1 tsp. light corn syrup, 1/4 tsp. pure vanilla extract, and 1/4 tsp. table salt with a mixer until combined. Beat in 4 oz. melted semisweet bar chocolate just until combined. Ice doughnuts immediately after making icing.

**RECIPE VARIATION:**
## Chocolate Old-Fashioned Doughnuts

Reduce baking powder to 3 tsp. Add $\frac{1}{8}$ tsp. baking soda. Omit mace. Combine $\frac{3}{4}$ cup unsweetened cocoa powder, sifted, $\frac{1}{2}$ cup hot water, and $\frac{1}{2}$ tsp. espresso powder until smooth. Add cocoa mixture to mixer after sour cream.

Per serving double-dipped in chocolate glaze: 752 cal; 26g total fat (8g sat); 75mg chol; 587mg sodium; 126g carb; 2g fiber; 8g protein

# Donut Muffins

These muffins offer a grown-up version of one of childhood's greatest pleasures — the variety six-pack of mini-donuts. Here they show up in the form of bite-sized muffins. You'll want to take time to savor these, and so will everyone who tastes them.

**TEST KITCHEN TIP:**
**Make-Ahead**

You can bake and cool muffins ahead without the toppings. Store the muffins in a plastic freezer bag in the freezer for up to 1 month. To serve, thaw muffins before topping.

# Variety-Pack Donut Muffins

*Coat the entire muffin pan, including the surface between the cups, with nonstick spray to prevent the muffin tops from sticking to the pan.*

Makes 48 mini muffins
Total time: about 35 minutes + cooling

**FOR THE MUFFINS, WHISK:**

| | |
|---|---|
| 3 | cups all-purpose flour |
| 2 | tsp. baking powder |
| 1 | tsp. table salt |
| 1 | tsp. ground nutmeg |
| 1/2 | tsp. baking soda |
| 1 1/4 | cups whole milk |
| 1/2 | cup sour cream |
| 1 1/2 | sticks unsalted butter, softened (12 Tbsp.) |
| 1/2 | cup granulated sugar |
| 1/3 | cup packed brown sugar |
| 2 | eggs |

**FOR THE CINNAMON-SUGAR, COMBINE:**

| | |
|---|---|
| 1 | cup granulated sugar |
| 1 | Tbsp. ground cinnamon |
| 1 | stick unsalted butter, melted (8 Tbsp.) |

**FOR THE POWDERED SUGAR, ROLL:**

| | |
|---|---|
| 1 | cup sifted powdered sugar |

**FOR THE CHOCOLATE GLAZE, HEAT:**

| | |
|---|---|
| 4 | Tbsp. unsalted butter |
| 3 | Tbsp. heavy cream |
| 1 | Tbsp. light corn syrup |
| 1 | tsp. pure vanilla extract |
| 2 | oz. bittersweet *or* semisweet bar chocolate, chopped |
| 1 | cup sifted powdered sugar |

**Preheat** oven to 350°. Coat mini muffin pans with nonstick spray.

**For the muffins, whisk** together flour, baking powder, salt, nutmeg, and baking soda. Combine milk and sour cream.

**Cream** butter, granulated sugar, and brown sugar in a bowl until light and fluffy.

**Beat in** eggs one at a time until fully incorporated.

**Alternately add** flour mixture and milk mixture to butter mixture, starting and ending with flour mixture. Mix batter until just combined and smooth.

**Transfer** a heaping 1-tablespoon batter into each well of prepared pans and bake muffins until a toothpick inserted in the centers comes out clean, 12–15 minutes. Cool muffins in the pans 5 minutes, then turn them out. Apply toppings while muffins are warm.

**For the cinnamon-sugar, combine** sugar and cinnamon. Dunk warm muffins first in melted butter, letting excess drip off, then roll in the cinnamon-sugar mixture.

**For the powdered sugar, roll** warm muffins in powdered sugar until completely coated.

**For the chocolate glaze, heat** butter, cream, corn syrup, and vanilla in a saucepan over low until butter melts. Whisk in chocolate until melted. Stir in powdered sugar until smooth. Dip tops of warm muffins with glaze

Per muffin with cinnamon-sugar topping: 100 cal; 5g total fat (3g sat); 22mg chol; 92mg sodium; 12g carb; 0g fiber; 1g protein

Adding the eggs one at a time ensures that they'll be fully incorporated into the batter.

To prevent tough muffins caused by overmixing, alternately add the dry and wet ingredients.

A tablespoon measure is ideal for forming mini muffins that don't have oversized lids.

# Sensational Scones

Rise and shine to these simple, make-ahead scones. All you'll have to do besides pop them in the oven is brew the coffee! Loaded with cranberries, pecans, a hint of orange, and served with a spiced orange marmalade, these scones ensure a sweet start to your day.

**TEST KITCHEN TIP:**
Make-Ahead

Arrange scones on baking sheet, cover with plastic wrap, and freeze overnight. (Omit egg wash if freezing longer than 30 minutes.) Make marmalade 3 days ahead.

# Cranberry-Pecan Scones
## with spiced orange marmalade

*Sanding or coarse sugar gives the scones texture. But if you don't have any, or can't find it, substitute with granulated sugar.*

Makes 8 scones, 1 cup marmalade
Total time: 45 minutes + freezing

**FOR THE SCONES, COMBINE:**

2³/4 cups all-purpose flour
1/2 cup granulated sugar
1 Tbsp. baking powder
1/2 tsp. table salt

**CUT IN:**

1 stick cold unsalted butter, cubed (8 Tbsp.)
1/2 cup chopped pecans, toasted
1/2 cup dried cranberries
2 Tbsp. minced orange zest

**WHISK:**

1/2 cup buttermilk
2 eggs

**COMBINE:**

1 Tbsp. sanding sugar
1 Tbsp. minced orange zest
1 egg + 1 Tbsp. buttermilk, lightly beaten

**FOR THE MARMALADE, COMBINE:**

1 cup purchased sweet orange marmalade
4 tsp. minced jalapeño (*optional*)
1/4 tsp. ground cinnamon

**Line** a baking sheet with parchment paper. Lightly flour a work surface.
**For the scones, combine** flour, granulated sugar, baking powder, and salt.
**Cut in** butter with a pastry blender until pea-sized. Add pecans, cranberries, and 2 Tbsp. zest; toss to combine.
**Whisk** together 1/2 cup buttermilk and 2 eggs, then stir into flour mixture just until combined.
(It is a wet dough. Do not overmix.)
**Transfer** dough to prepared work surface; shape into an 8-inch round with lightly floured hands. Cut dough into 8 wedges; transfer to prepared baking sheet, spacing at least 1-inch apart.
**Combine** sanding sugar and 1 Tbsp. zest. Lightly brush tops of scones with egg wash; sprinkle with sugar-zest mixture. Freeze scones, uncovered, 30 minutes.
**Preheat** oven to 375°.
**Bake** scones until golden and set, 20–25 minutes. Let scones cool briefly on baking sheet; serve warm or at room temperature.
**For the marmalade, combine** marmalade, jalapeño, and cinnamon; serve with scones.

Per scone: 386 cal; 19g total fat (9g sat); 102mg chol; 398mg sodium; 50g carb; 2g fiber; 8g protein

For tender and flaky scones, a pastry blender cuts the butter into the flour without warming it.

To keep the scones from becoming tough, use very little flour on your hands and work surface.

For shiny scones, brush the tops with an egg wash. Space them apart so they rise evenly when baking.

# Best-Ever Biscuits

Dust off your biscuit cutter and get the butter ready —
flaky, tender biscuits are just minutes away! Using
a stand mixer puts these biscuits in the fast lane. Even
grandma would be proud, especially when you serve
them with the apricot butter on page 25.

**TEST KITCHEN TIP:**
Chill Factor

For biscuits with major
rise, pop any tools,
especially the stand mixer
bowl, into the freezer for
a few minutes before
mixing to ensure the fats
won't melt before baking.

## Basic Buttermilk Biscuits

*To avoid overmixing this biscuit dough, stop when the ingredients are just moistened. Even though it's a wet dough, don't be tempted to add more flour.*

Makes 10 biscuits
Total time: 30 minutes

| | |
|---|---|
| 1½ | cups all-purpose flour |
| 2 | tsp. baking powder |
| ½ | tsp. table salt |
| ¼ | tsp. baking soda |
| 1½ | cups cake flour |
| 5 | Tbsp. cold shortening, cubed |
| 4 | Tbsp. cold unsalted butter, cubed |
| 1¼ | cups buttermilk |
| 2 | Tbsp. unsalted butter, melted |

**Preheat** oven to 450°. Line a baking sheet with parchment paper.

**Whisk** together all-purpose flour, baking powder, salt, and baking soda in a bowl.

**Pulse** cake flour, shortening, and cubed butter in the bowl of a stand mixer with the paddle attachment until fats are pea-sized flakes. Mix in all-purpose flour mixture just until blended. Add buttermilk and mix just until moistened.

**Turn** dough onto a lightly floured surface, and knead just until dough holds together. Pat dough into a 1-inch-thick circle. Using a 2-inch biscuit cutter, cut dough into 10 biscuits. Transfer biscuits to prepared baking sheet and bake until golden, 15–18 minutes. Brush tops with melted butter during last few minutes of baking.

Per biscuit: 262 cal; 13g total fat (6g sat); 19mg chol; 279mg sodium; 31g carb; 1g fiber; 5g protein

Using the paddle attachment, mix dough until ingredients are just moistened.

Flour your hands to keep the dough from sticking, then pat the dough into a 1-inch-thick circle.

Pull cutter up, without twisting — twisting prevents the biscuits from rising to their full potential.

## Apricot Pecan Butter

*Biscuits are a southern tradition and a praline butter is a fitting stand-in for jams and jellies. Peaches can be substituted for the apricots.*

Makes about 2 cups
Total time: 20 minutes

| | |
|---|---|
| 4 | Tbsp. unsalted butter |
| 2½ | cups sliced fresh apricots |
| ½ | cup apricot preserves |
| ⅓ | cup packed brown sugar |
| ½ | tsp. pure vanilla extract |
| ¼ | tsp. ground cinnamon |
| 2 | Tbsp. heavy cream |
| 1 | Tbsp. rum (*optional*) |
| ½ | cup chopped pecans, toasted |

**Melt** butter in a sauté pan over medium heat. Add apricots and cook, stirring occasionally until softened, about 5 minutes.

**Stir in** preserves and brown sugar until melted. Add vanilla and cinnamon, bring to a boil, and boil without stirring 3–5 minutes.

**Off heat, whisk in** cream and rum (the mixture will sputter), then add pecans.

**Serve** apricot butter warm with biscuits, or store in an airtight container and refrigerate for up to 1 week.

Per 2 Tbsp.: 114 cal; 6g total fat (2g sat); 10mg chol; 3mg sodium; 14g carb; 1g fiber; 1g protein

# HOT OFF
# THE GRIDDLE

Put on some coffee. It's time to heat the griddle and get cookin' with recipes that are sure to satisfy.

# Ricotta Pancakes

Nothing says weekends, or holidays, more than pancakes for breakfast, especially these delicate, airy ones. And with three sensational syrups, you have every reason to celebrate.

There's a secret ingredient in this batter — ricotta cheese — but you don't actually taste the cheese. Basically the ricotta melts into the batter as the pancakes cook, adding luxurious creaminess to these flapjacks.

Other than the addition of ricotta, a little sugar, vanilla, and lemon zest add just the right amount of flavor.

## Ricotta Pancakes

*These pancakes taste so good and are so easy to whip together, you'll likely want declare every day pancake day!*

Makes 6 servings (12 pancakes); Total time: 30 minutes

**WHISK:**
- 3/4  cup all-purpose flour
- 1  tsp. baking powder
- 1/2  tsp. table salt

**WHISK:**
- 1  cup whole milk ricotta cheese
- 1/2  cup whole milk
- 2  Tbsp. sugar
- 2  Tbsp. unsalted butter, melted and slightly cooled
- 2  eggs, separated
- 1/2  tsp. pure vanilla extract
  Minced zest of 1/2 a lemon

**Whisk** together flour, baking powder, and salt in a large bowl, then form a well in the center.

**Whisk** together ricotta, milk, sugar, butter, egg yolks, vanilla, and zest in a large measuring cup; pour into dry ingredients, stirring just until incorporated.

**Whip** egg whites with a hand mixer on high speed until stiff peaks form, 2–3 minutes.

**Stir** one third of egg whites into the batter; fold in remaining whites in two additions.

**Heat** an electric griddle to 375° or a nonstick skillet over medium; coat with nonstick spray. Drop half the batter, by a scant 1/4 cup per pancake, onto griddle; cook until bubbles appear on tops and bottoms brown, 4 minutes. Flip pancakes and cook until bottoms brown, 3 minutes more. Repeat with remaining batter.

Per serving: 205 cal; 11g total fat (7g sat); 95mg chol; 353mg sodium; 17g carb; 0g fiber; 9g protein

So the melted butter doesn't "cook" the cheese, milk, or yolks, cool it slightly before adding it.

Pouring the wet ingredients into a well in the dry ingredients allows for quicker, easier mixing.

Stir in some egg whites to lighten the batter, then fold in the rest in batches so as not to deflate them too much.

# Top it off

Ricotta pancakes are definitely something special, and even better when you top them with one of these three syrups. A New Orleans-inspired syrup, a sweet-and-sour berry sauce, and a brunch drink turned into a topper will make your morning so much tastier. Based on Louisiana's trademark confection, the praline, this caramel-based syrup has so much going for it. With warm spices and loads of pecans, you'll want to make extra to spoon over everything.

**Pecan Praline
Pancake Syrup**
with fresh pineapple

*Brown sugar makes for a thicker sauce, but if you're a maple syrup fan, substitute it for the sugar and you'll be just as happy.*

Makes about 1¾ cups
Total time: 20 minutes

**MELT:**

| 1 | stick unsalted butter (8 Tbsp.) |
| 1 | cup packed brown sugar *or* pure maple syrup |

**WHISK IN:**

| ½ | cup heavy cream |
| ½ | tsp. ground allspice |
| ½ | tsp. table salt |

**STIR IN:**

| ¾ | cup chopped pecans, toasted |
| 2 | Tbsp. spiced rum, bourbon, *or* pineapple juice |
| 1 | tsp. pure vanilla extract |
| | Fresh pineapple wedges |

**Melt** butter with brown sugar in a saucepan over medium heat, whisking constantly until smooth, about 2 minutes.

**Whisk in** cream, allspice, and salt; bring to a boil, then reduce heat to medium-low, and simmer until sauce thickens, about 5 minutes.

**Stir in** pecans, rum, and vanilla.

**Serve** syrup over pancakes with pineapple wedges.

Per ¼ cup: 387 cal; 28g total fat (13g sat); 58mg chol; 183mg sodium; 33g carb; 1g fiber; 2g protein

## Peach Bellini Pancake Syrup

Makes about 1¾ cups
Total time: 20 minutes

**HEAT:**

| | |
|---|---|
| 8 | oz. frozen sliced peaches (generous 1 cup) |
| 1 | cup Prosecco |
| ½ | cup peach nectar, divided |
| 3 | Tbsp. sugar |

**WHISK:**

| | |
|---|---|
| 1 | Tbsp. cornstarch |
| 1 | tsp. fresh lemon juice |
| ⅛ | tsp. table salt |
| | Whole milk ricotta cheese |
| | Fresh raspberries |

**Heat** peaches, Prosecco, ¼ cup peach nectar, and sugar in a saucepan over medium-high to a boil. Reduce heat to medium and simmer, stirring occasionally, until syrup is slightly reduced and peaches are tender, 12–15 minutes. **Whisk** together remaining ¼ cup peach nectar and cornstarch, then whisk into syrup and cook until it thickens, 2–3 minutes; stir in lemon juice and salt.

**Serve** syrup over pancakes with a dollop of ricotta and raspberries.

Per ¼ cup: 61 cal; 0g total fat (0g sat); 0mg chol; 45mg sodium; 11g carb; 1g fiber; 0g protein

## Blueberry Agrodolce Pancake Syrup

*Fresh or frozen blueberries both work in this syrup. If using frozen, just be sure to thaw a half cup of the berries to add at the end.*

Makes about 1¾ cups
Total time: 20 minutes

**HEAT:**

| | |
|---|---|
| 2½ | cups fresh *or* frozen blueberries, divided |
| ⅓ | cup *each* sugar and water |
| 2 | sprigs fresh thyme |
| 1 | cinnamon stick (3-inch) |

**OFF HEAT, STIR IN:**

| | |
|---|---|
| 2 | Tbsp. unsalted butter |
| 1 | Tbsp. white wine *or* Champagne vinegar |
| ¼ | tsp. table salt |

**Heat** 2 cups blueberries, sugar, water, thyme, and cinnamon in a saucepan over medium-high to a boil. Reduce heat to medium-low and simmer, stirring occasionally, until syrup begins to thicken, 7–9 minutes.

**Off heat, stir in** butter and vinegar until butter melts; stir in remaining ½ cup blueberries and salt.

**Serve** syrup over pancakes.

Per ¼ cup: 82 cal; 3g total fat (2g sat); 9mg chol; 84mg sodium; 14g carb; 1g fiber; 0g protein

# Swedish Pancakes

If you've never tried this Scandinavian breakfast favorite, these Swedish delights are a treat that everyone at your brunch table will flip over. Not your typical flapjack, they're super thin and similar to crêpes because they have more eggs and melted butter than flour. And with no baking powder or baking soda, these pancakes don't puff. Instead, beaten egg whites give them a silky-smooth texture.

## Classic Swedish Pancakes

*Though traditionally topped with nothing more than lingonberry jam and powdered sugar, try these pancakes with your favorite jellies and jams.*

Makes 8–12 pancakes
Total time: 1 hour

| | |
|---|---|
| 3 | eggs, separated |
| 1 | cup whole milk |
| 4 | Tbsp. unsalted butter, melted |
| 2 | Tbsp. sugar |
| 1 | tsp. pure vanilla extract |
| 1/4 | tsp. table salt |
| 1 | cup all-purpose flour |
| | Unsalted butter |

**Preheat** oven to 200°.

**Beat** egg whites in a bowl with a hand mixer on medium speed to stiff peaks; set aside.

**Whisk** egg yolks, milk, melted butter, sugar, vanilla, and salt in a bowl until combined. Add flour and whisk just until combined.

**Fold in** beaten egg whites.

**Melt** 1–2 tsp. butter in a 10-inch nonstick skillet over medium-low heat until foamy.

**Scoop** 1/3 to 1/2 cup batter into skillet and tilt to let batter run to edges, covering entire bottom (or spread with the back of a dinner spoon). When top of pancake looks dry, loosen edges with a rubber spatula and flip. Cook pancakes until golden, 1–2 minutes per side. Transfer pancakes to a baking sheet and keep warm in oven while repeating with remaining batter.

Per pancake with cream cheese filling and blueberry sauce: 222 cal; 13g total fat (7g sat); 89mg chol; 137mg sodium; 23g carb; 1g fiber; 5g protein

Swirl batter to cover entire bottom of skillet. If it doesn't run, spread it with the back of a spoon to cover.

The pancakes are very pliable and should be easy to flip, but use your hand to help support them.

**RECIPE VARIATIONS:**
## Pancake Change-Ups

• **LEMON POPPY SEED PANCAKES** Stir 1 Tbsp. *each* minced lemon zest, fresh lemon juice, and poppy seeds into the batter.

• **CREAM CHEESE FILLING** Beat 8 oz. softened cream cheese, 2 Tbsp. whole milk, 1 Tbsp. sugar, 1 tsp. pure vanilla extract, and 1/8 tsp. ground nutmeg in a bowl with hand mixer on medium speed until combined, then divide among pancakes and roll to serve.

• **BLUEBERRY SAUCE** Boil 2 cups blueberries, 1/2 cup water, and 1/3 cup sugar in a saucepan over medium heat until it begins to thicken, about 10 minutes. Whisk together 1 Tbsp. water and 1 tsp. cornstarch for a slurry in a small bowl, stir into sauce, and cook 1 minute to thicken. Stir in 1/2 cup fresh blueberries and serve over pancakes.

# Baked French Toast

When you have a group to feed and want to keep things simple, this baked French toast is just the ticket. There's no standing over a hot griddle calling "order up!" With this baked version, all the pieces are done at the same time and everyone gets to enjoy breakfast together.

**GOOD TO KNOW:**
Maple Syrup

Maple syrup is made by reducing the maple sap into a sweeter, more concentrated form. On average, it takes 40 gallons of maple sap to produce 1 gallon of syrup.

## Spiced Orange Baked French Toast
### with maple-orange syrup

*By assembling the French toast and shaping the sausages the night before, all you have to do in the morning is bake the French toast and fry the sausages.*

Makes 6 servings (12 pieces)
Total time: 30 minutes + soaking

**COAT:**

| | |
|---|---|
| 4 | Tbsp. unsalted butter, melted |

**FOR THE FRENCH TOAST, COMBINE:**

| | |
|---|---|
| 6 | eggs, beaten |
| 1¹/₂ | cups *each* whole milk and heavy cream |
| ¹/₄ | cup granulated sugar |
| ¹/₄ | cup orange liqueur (such as Grand Marnier) |
| 1 | tsp. ground mace |
| 12 | slices challah bread, 1- to 1¹/₄-inches thick (about 1 loaf) |

**FOR THE SYRUP, SIMMER:**

| | |
|---|---|
| 1 | cup pure maple syrup |
| 3 | Tbsp. fresh orange juice |
| 1 | Tbsp. unsalted butter |
| | Pinch of salt |
| 1 | tsp. pure vanilla extract |
| | Toasted sliced almonds |
| | Powdered sugar |

**Coat** a large baking sheet with melted butter.

**For the French toast, combine** eggs, milk, cream, granulated sugar, orange liqueur, and mace.

**Dip** bread into egg mixture to coat both sides. Arrange slices on prepared baking sheet in a single layer. Pour remaining egg mixture over the top; refrigerate, covered, 2 hours or overnight.

**Preheat** oven to 475°. Bring chilled slices to room temperature.

**Bake** French toast 7–8 minutes, flip, and bake until puffed and golden, 7–8 minutes more. Broil French toast on high with rack 6 inches from element until it begins to brown, about 3 minutes.

**For the syrup, simmer** maple syrup, juice, butter, and salt in a saucepan. Off heat, whisk in vanilla.

**Serve** French toast with syrup and garnish with almonds and powdered sugar.

Per serving: 670 cal; 39g total fat (22g sat); 302mg chol; 314mg sodium; 63g carb; 1g fiber; 15g protein

## Homemade Breakfast Sausage Patties

*Making homemade sausages is a snap. Once you've tried them, you may never go back to store-bought.*

Makes 6 servings (12 patties)
Total time: 20 minutes + chilling

| | |
|---|---|
| 1 | lb. ground pork |
| 1 | Tbsp. brown sugar |
| 1¹/₂ | tsp. minced fresh garlic |
| 1¹/₂ | tsp. ground sage |
| 1 | tsp. kosher salt |
| 1 | tsp. fennel seeds |
| ¹/₂ | tsp. red pepper flakes |
| ¹/₂ | tsp. freshly grated nutmeg |

**Combine** pork, brown sugar, garlic, sage, salt, fennel seeds, pepper flakes, and nutmeg in a bowl.

**Divide** sausage mixture in half and shape each half into a log. Wrap logs in plastic wrap and chill until slightly firm, at least 1 hour or overnight.

**Unwrap** logs and slice into twelve patties, reshaping as necessary.

**Fry** patties in a large nonstick skillet coated with nonstick spray over medium-high heat until cooked through, 5–7 minutes per side. Transfer patties to a paper-towel-lined plate.

Per serving: 211 cal; 16g total fat (6g sat); 54mg chol; 363mg sodium; 3g carb; 0g fiber; 13g protein

To minimize sticking, be sure to coat the whole baking sheet (sides and corners) with melted butter.

Evenly pour the remaining egg mixture over slices. The bread will absorb it while chilling.

# Swiss Eibrot

Simple, sweet, and Swiss — this heirloom recipe has been passed down for generations. These little golden bites are similar to French toast, but tossed in a butter-sugar glaze, they taste like a million bucks.

## Swiss Eibrot

*For the best results, cook the eibrot in two batches. Overcrowding the pan steams the bread, batches ensure that each cube develops a golden crust.*

Makes 6 servings (6 cups)
Total time: 40 minutes

**WHISK:**

| | |
|---|---|
| 5 | eggs |
| 2 | cups whole milk |
| 1 | tsp. pure vanilla extract |
| 1/4 | tsp. ground cinnamon |

**TOSS IN:**

| | |
|---|---|
| 8 | cups 1-inch cubed bread (such as challah, French bread, *or* sourdough) |
| 6 | Tbsp. vegetable oil |
| 6 | Tbsp. unsalted butter |
| 1 | cup sugar |

**Whisk** together eggs, milk, vanilla, and cinnamon in a bowl.

**Toss in** 4 cups bread, allow bread to sit until the cubes are thoroughly soaked, about 5 minutes.

**Heat** 3 Tbsp. oil in a large nonstick skillet over medium-high. Sauté soaked bread in a single layer, stirring occasionally, until golden, about 8 minutes.

**Meanwhile, soak** remaining bread in remaining egg mixture.

**Add** 3 Tbsp. butter to sautéed bread; stir until butter melts and bread is coated.

**Sprinkle** 1/2 cup sugar over bread in skillet; toss until sugar melts and is syrupy. Transfer eibrot to a platter, then serve.

**Repeat** sautéing the remaining bread using the remaining 3 Tbsp. oil, 3 Tbsp. butter, and 1/2 cup sugar. Transfer eibrot to the platter, then serve.

Per serving: 561 calories; 33g total fat (11g sat); 193mg chol; 452mg sodium; 57g carb; 2g fiber; 12g protein

Whisk eggs, milk, vanilla, and cinnamon together. A large bowl is necessary to fit all the bread.

You want to make sure the bread cubes absorb the egg mixture — allow them to sit until soaked.

To ensure each bread cube gets crisp, sauté them in a single layer in batches.

## Sugar & Spice Bacon

*You can easily double or triple this recipe as needed — or as you like — trust us, you'll want to.*

Makes 8 strips
Total time: 20 minutes

**COOK:**

| | |
|---|---|
| 8 | strips thick-sliced bacon |

**ADD:**

| | |
|---|---|
| 2 | Tbsp. brown sugar |
| 1 | Tbsp. red wine vinegar |
| 1/4 | tsp. cayenne pepper |

**Cook** bacon in a nonstick skillet until crisp; transfer to a paper-towel-lined plate and pour off drippings.

**Add** sugar, vinegar, and cayenne to skillet; simmer over medium heat, 30 seconds. Reduce heat to low, return bacon to skillet, and toss until coated with glaze.

Per strip: 71 cal; 5g total fat (2g sat); 10mg chol; 250mg sodium; 3g carb; 0g fiber; 4g protein

# Hash Brown Heaven

Transform a plain — but much-loved — potato side dish into a crisp and buttery main event. Stuffed with the king of fresh vegetables, plus rich and creamy Brie cheese, this dish is satisfying morning, noon, or night, and it's just the right amount for a simple meal for two.

**GOOD TO KNOW:**
Brie Cheese

Characterized by its edible, downy white rind and cream-colored, buttery-soft interior, Brie is touted as one of the world's greatest cheeses, especially Brie from France.

## Hash Brown "Omelet"
### with asparagus & brie

*This recipe easily doubles. Make them one at a time, or use two skillets.*

Makes 2 servings
Total time: 30 minutes

**FOR THE FILLING, SIMMER:**

1/2    cup asparagus tips

**WHIP:**

1/2    cup Brie cheese (4 oz.), rind removed and softened
1      Tbsp. heavy cream *or half-and-half*
1      Tbsp. minced fresh chives
       Salt and black pepper to taste

**FOR THE POTATOES, HEAT:**

1      Tbsp. peanut oil
2      Tbsp. unsalted butter

**ADD:**

1      lb. russet potatoes, peeled, shredded, rinsed, and dried

**For the filling, simmer** asparagus in a skillet with water to cover until crisp-tender, 3 minutes. Drain asparagus and rinse with cold water until cool to the touch.

**Whip** Brie and cream in a bowl with a hand mixer until light and fluffy. Stir in chives; season with salt and pepper.

**For the potatoes, heat** oil in a skillet over medium-high until shimmering. Add 1 Tbsp. butter until melted and foam subsides, swirling skillet to keep butter from burning.

**Add** potatoes; press with a spatula into a disk.

**Cook** potatoes (without stirring) until golden on the edges, 7–8 minutes.

**Slide** hash browns onto a large plate, cover with another plate, then invert so browned side is up.

**Melt** remaining 1 Tbsp. butter in skillet over medium-high heat. Slide hash browns back into skillet, browned side up; cook until golden brown, 5–6 minutes.

**Arrange** asparagus on half the hash browns, then spoon half of the Brie mixture over top, and season with salt and pepper.

**Fold** the unfilled hash browns over the filling; let stand 1 minute until cheese melts and asparagus warms.

**Cut** omelet in half. Top servings with a remaining whipped Brie.

Per serving: 561 cal; 37g total fat (20g sat); 97mg chol; 373mg sodium; 43g carb; 4g fiber; 18g protein

## Fruit Cocktail
### with lime-mint syrup

*This refreshing fruit salad is a palate cleanser. It's perfect with the omelet, and one you'll want to keep on hand.*

Makes 4 servings (5 cups)
Total time: 15 minutes

**WHISK:**

       Minced zest of 1 lime
1/4    cup fresh lime juice
1      Tbsp. chopped fresh mint
1      Tbsp. honey

**TOSS:**

2      cups cubed cantaloupe
2      cups halved seedless red *and/or* green grapes
1–2    bananas, sliced
       Fresh mint sprigs

**Whisk** together zest, lime juice, chopped mint, and honey in a bowl until dissolved.

**Toss** cantaloupe and grapes with lime mixture. Stir in banana just before serving. Garnish servings with mint sprigs.

Per serving: 128 cal; 0g total fat (0g sat); 0mg chol; 15mg sodium; 33g carb; 2g fiber; 2g protein

To easily whip the Brie, first remove the rind while it's chilled, then let it come to room temperature.

Use two plates to quickly flip the hash browns so the cooked side is up, then slide back into the skillet.

# One Potato

Hash browns have been on menus in mom-and-pop cafes for generations. And depending upon where you grew up, shredded or cubed potatoes are the true hash browns. But any way you cut it, these recipes are the real deal.

## Golden Hash Browns

Makes 4 servings
Total time: 25 minutes

**HEAT:**

1    Tbsp. peanut oil
2    Tbsp. unsalted butter

**ADD:**

1    lb. russet potatoes, peeled, shredded, rinsed, and dried
     Salt and black pepper to taste

**Heat** oil in a medium skillet over medium-high until shimmering. Add 1 Tbsp. butter until melted and foam subsides, swirling skillet to keep butter from burning.
**Add** potatoes; press with a spatula into a disk.

**Cook** potatoes (without stirring) until golden brown on the edges, 7–8 minutes.
**Slide** hash browns onto a large plate, cover with another plate, then invert so the browned side is up.
**Melt** remaining 1 Tbsp. butter in skillet over medium-high heat. Slide hash browns back into skillet, browned side up; cook until golden brown, 5–6 minutes. Season hash browns with salt and pepper.

Per serving: 170 cal; 9g total fat (4g sat); 15mg chol; 126mg sodium; 21g carb; 1g fiber; 2g protein

For crisp hash browns, dry potatoes well. A paper-towel-lined salad spinner makes it quick and easy.

Firmly press the potato shreds to form a cake and expose the most surface area for crisp browning.

# Two Potatoes

Starchy, low-moisture spuds, like golds or russets, are what you're looking for. And for the best flavor, and browning, use two fats — peanut oil and butter are the way to go.

## Country-Style Hash Browns

*Golden potatoes have enough starch to stand up as cubes when frying. Plus, they look and taste great.*

Makes 4 servings
Total time: 25 minutes

- 1    Tbsp. peanut oil
- 1    Tbsp. unsalted butter
- 1    lb. Yukon gold *or* russet potatoes, peeled, 1/2-inch diced, soaked, rinsed, and dried
       Salt and black pepper to taste

**Heat** oil in a medium skillet over medium-high until shimmering. Add butter until melted and foam subsides, swirling skillet to keep butter from burning.
**Add** potatoes and cook (without stirring) until golden brown on the edges, 8–10 minutes.
**Stir** hash browns and cook until all sides are golden brown, 8–10 minutes more, stirring occasionally; season with salt and pepper.

Per serving: 145 cal; 6g total fat (2g sat); 8mg chol; 126mg sodium; 21g carb; 1g fiber; 2g protein

For uniform-sized potatoes, cut into 1/2-inch planks, then lengthwise into strips, and last, slice across to dice.

**GOOD TO KNOW:**
## Yukon Golds

The result of crossbreeding a white potato with a yellow-fleshed variety, this waxy, pale, firm potato is great for roasting, frying, and mashing.

# THE EGGS
# HAVE IT!

These recipes show you how to whip the humble egg into a variety of dishes in no time at all.

# ALL ABOUT EGGS

**LET'S FACE IT,** eggs serve so many functions in the kitchen, it's practically impossible to cook without them. Plus, they're nutrition-packed, economical, and readily available — it's no wonder they're considered incredible. And with this primer, there's no need to scramble your brain on how to prepare them to perfection every time.

## TOOLS WE LIKE

### Trusty Nonstick Skillet

Never struggle with omelets or fried eggs again. This 8-inch skillet from Circulon has an aluminum core and a stainless-steel base that make it perfect for use on all stove tops. The sloped sides allow you to flip omelets like a pro. $25, www.circulon.com

## SPECIALTY EGGS

When you shop for eggs, your choices include more than just jumbo or large. Organic eggs are produced by hens that haven't been given feed containing pesticides, growth hormones, or antibiotics. Nutrient-enhanced eggs contain increased amounts of Omega-3 fatty acids or lutein. These eggs come from hens that have been fed an enriched diet. You may find some specialty eggs certified by the United Egg Producers, who guarantee that strict animal-welfare standards have been met in the care and handling of egg-laying hens.

# HOW TO COOK THE PERFECT EGG

**Scrambled:** Heat a nonstick skillet over medium-high; add 2 tsp. butter. Whisk together 2 eggs and 2 Tbsp. milk; add to skillet. Pull a spatula through eggs to create large curds; cook about 2 minutes.

**Hard-cooked:** Place eggs in a saucepan; add cold water to cover by 1 inch. Bring eggs to a boil, cover, remove from heat, and let sit 10 minutes. Transfer eggs to a bowl of cold water to stop the cooking.

**Fried:** Heat a nonstick skillet over medium; add 2 tsp. butter. Crack 2 eggs into skillet. Cook until egg white nearest yolk turns opaque. Flip eggs; cook another 30 seconds for over-easy, about 3 minutes total.

**Poached:** Bring 6 cups water and 3 Tbsp. vinegar to a simmer in a sauté pan. Carefully slip eggs into the water, one at a time. Cook to desired doneness, 4 to 6 minutes. Use a strainer to remove eggs from the pan.

### Versatile Butterfly Whisk

Unusual butterfly-shaped wires in this whisk by Kuhn Rikon are designed especially for whipping eggs. Silicon coating makes this whisk safe for use in nonstick pans. And it tolerates high heat. $20, www.kuhnrikonshop.com

## KEEP 'EM SEPARATED

Here's how we like to separate eggs. First, crack an egg on the countertop. Next, transfer yolk between halves of shell (or use an egg separator) over a small bowl, allowing white to fall into the bowl. Put the yolk in another bowl. Transfer individual whites from a small bowl to a larger collection bowl. If any yolk makes its way into an egg white, only that one white will be ruined.

### 3-Way Egg Slicer

This three-in-one slicer by Amco Houseworks features two cutting discs so you can slice, dice, and cut perfect wedges with ease. The rubberized base keeps it in place while using. $15, www.amcohouseworks.com

**Omelet with Spinach-Artichoke Filling**
see pages 47–48

# Mastering French Omelets

If you can scramble eggs, you can make omelets — and one of the fastest and easiest methods is the stirred (and shaken) French omelet. But note, the omelets should be pale with no browning. Also, this method yields a tender omelet with a creamy center that's set but still looks wet when you add your filling, which will get nicely tucked inside once folded.

## Basic Omelet

*Check out the filling suggestions on pages 48–49. And make sure your fillings are fully prepared before you crack an egg.*

Makes 1 omelet
Total time: 10 minutes

| | |
|---|---|
| 3 | eggs |
| 2 | Tbsp. half-and-half, milk, *or* water |
| 1 | Tbsp. unsalted butter |
| | Salt and black pepper |
| 1/4–1/3 | cup desired filling (*pages 48–49*) |

**Whisk** together eggs and half-and-half in a bowl.

**Melt** butter in an 8-inch nonstick skillet over medium-high heat until bubbling.

**Pour** egg mixture into skillet and season with salt and pepper. Immediately begin gently shaking the skillet back and forth while making small, quick stirring motions. Reduce heat to low when eggs no longer run but are still moist.

**Add** filling in a line perpendicular to the skillet handle. Fold one-third of the omelet over the filling, then slide the exposed third of the omelet from the edge of the pan onto a serving plate, folding the rest of the omelet over on it. Let omelet rest 1 minute before serving.

Per omelet: 338 cal; 24g total fat (11g sat); 573mg chol; 344mg sodium; 6g carb; 0g fiber; 20g protein

## Master Technique: Tools & Steps

For guaranteed success, a nonstick skillet is essential. An 8- to 10-inch skillet is ideal for a three-egg omelet — any smaller and the omelet is too thick to fold; any bigger and the omelet is likely to be very thin and stick to the skillet.

**1. Simultaneously shake the skillet forward and back while stirring the eggs vigorously. When the edges are set, tilt the skillet to roll any still-liquid eggs to the edges to set.**

**2. Once all the eggs are set but still moist on top, sprinkle your chosen filling perpendicular to the skillet handle (this makes folding easier in the next step).**

**3. Loosen the eggs around the edge, hold the skillet with an underhand grip (tilting it up), and fold the back third of the omelet over the filling.**

**4. Slide the exposed third of the omelet off the edge of the skillet onto a plate. Fold the rest of the omelet over on it. Let the omelet rest one minute before serving.**

# Fill 'er up

Spinach and artichoke is a much-loved, classic pairing, while huevos rancheros is a popular breakfast dish on its own — both make wonderful omelet fillings. Just remember to keep the size of the pieces on the smaller side, so the omelets are easier to fold and less likely to tear when folding.

Looking for more ideas? Here's some food for thought. From the more expected — Herb & Cheese, Denver, or Greek — to the more unique — BLT or California, give one of these other filling ideas a try. Or come up with your own combos — the options are truly endless.

## ENDLESS OMELET POSSIBILITIES

**BLT** Summer's favorite sandwich gets a new look. Simply fold cooked bacon, chopped tomatoes, and shredded lettuce into your next omelet.

**CALIFORNIA** Lump crab meat, chopped avocado, and a squeeze of lime juice reign supreme in these fresh, beachy omelets.

**DENVER** This western classic is on every breakfast menu. Diced ham, onion, bell pepper, and cheese are totally at home on the range in these omelets.

**GREEK** Feta cheese, cherry tomatoes, fresh oregano, and a little lemon zest give any omelet wonderful Mediterranean flair.

**HERB & CHEESE** Add your favorite cheese like goat, Cheddar, or Parmesan with a sprinkling of chopped fresh chives, parsley, chervil, and tarragon.

## Spinach-Artichoke Filling

*This recipe makes enough to fill six omelets. But be sure you make the filling before making the omelets.*

Makes 6 servings
Total time: 20 minutes

**SWEAT:**

| | |
|---|---|
| 1/2 | cup diced onion |
| 1 | Tbsp. *each* olive oil and unsalted butter |
| 1 | Tbsp. minced fresh garlic |
| 1/4 | tsp. red pepper flakes |
| 1 | can quartered artichoke hearts (13.75 oz.), drained |

**ADD:**

| | |
|---|---|
| 4 | oz. cream cheese |
| 1/4 | cup heavy cream |
| 2 | Tbsp. *each* chopped fresh chives, dill, and parsley |
| | Minced zest of 1 lemon |

**STIR IN:**

| | |
|---|---|
| 3 | cups fresh spinach |
| | Salt and black pepper to taste |

**Sweat** onion in oil and butter in a sauté pan over medium-low heat until it begins to soften, 5 minutes. Add garlic and pepper flakes; cook 1 minute. Stir in artichoke hearts until warmed through.

**Add** cream cheese and cream, stirring until cream cheese melts, then stir in chives, dill, parsley, and zest.

**Stir in** spinach and cook until it begins to wilt; season with salt and pepper.

**Prepare and fill** omelets according to recipe directions, *page 47*.

Per serving: 175 cal; 14g total fat (8g sat); 40mg chol; 248mg sodium; 8g carb; 1g fiber; 4g protein

# Huevos Rancheros Omelets

*Breakfast sausage and cheese fill these omelets, while salsa and beans round out the plate for a hearty breakfast. For a dinner option, you might swap chorizo for the sausage.*

Makes 4 servings
Total time: 20 minutes

### FOR THE FILLING, BROWN:

| | |
|---|---|
| 8 | oz. bulk breakfast sausage |
| 1 | cup shredded pepper Jack cheese |

### FOR THE SAUCE, HEAT:

| | |
|---|---|
| 2 | cups purchased salsa |
| 1 | can black beans (15 oz.), drained and rinsed |
| 1/4 | cup chopped fresh cilantro |

### FOR THE OMELETS, WHISK:

| | |
|---|---|
| 12 | eggs, divided |
| 4 | Tbsp. sour cream, divided |
| | Sour cream |
| | Chopped fresh cilantro |

**For the filling, brown** sausage in a skillet over medium-high; transfer to a paper-towel-lined plate.

**For the sauce, heat** salsa and beans in a saucepan over medium until warmed through. Stir in 1/4 cup cilantro, reduce heat to low, and keep sauce warm.

**For the omelets, whisk** together 3 eggs and 1 Tbsp. sour cream for one omelet; cook according to directions, *page 47*, filling with one-fourth *each* sausage and cheese.

**Spoon** one-fourth sauce onto a serving plate, top with omelet, a dollop of sour cream, and chopped cilantro. Repeat procedures to make three more omelets.

Per omelet: 747 cal; 50g total fat (22g sat); 646mg chol; 1270mg sodium; 28g carb; 5g fiber; 40g protein

THE EGGS
**HAVE IT!**

# Rise And Dine

When cooking for an early morning crowd, these make-ahead cheesy, slightly spicy scrambled eggs are pure gold. All you have to do is pop this "hands-off" baked dish into the oven, brew some coffee, and you're ready to roll — you'll actually have time to put your feet up.

**GOOD TO KNOW:**
**Make-Ahead Tips**

After pouring the egg-pepper-cheese mixture into the prepared baking dish, cover with plastic wrap and refrigerate overnight (be sure to uncover before baking).

# Cheesy Scrambled Egg Bake

*If you prefer more subtle-flavored eggs, you can swap out the pepper Jack cheese for Monterey Jack, and seed your jalapeño.*

Makes 8 servings
Total time: 45 minutes

**COAT:**

| | |
|---|---|
| 4 | Tbsp. unsalted butter, divided |
| 1 | cup diced red bell peppers |
| 1/4 | cup minced scallion whites |
| 2 | Tbsp. minced jalapeño |

**WHISK:**

| | |
|---|---|
| 16 | eggs |
| 1 | cup heavy cream |
| 1 1/2 | tsp. kosher salt |
| 1 | tsp. black pepper |
| 1 1/2 | cups shredded pepper Jack cheese |
| 1/2 | cup thinly sliced scallion greens |

To keep the eggs from curdling, be sure to let the peppers mixture cool before adding it to the egg mixture.

**Preheat** oven to 350°.

**Coat** a 9×13-inch baking dish with 2 Tbsp. melted butter.

**Melt** remaining 2 Tbsp. butter in a nonstick skillet over medium heat. Add bell peppers, scallion whites, and jalapeño to skillet; cook until softened, about 5 minutes, then let cool to room temperature.

**Whisk** together eggs, cream, salt, and black pepper. Stir bell pepper mixture, cheese, and scallion greens into egg mixture; pour into prepared baking dish.

**Bake** egg mixture 10 minutes; stir and bake until eggs are set to your liking, 10–20 minutes more. Transfer eggs to a serving bowl.

Because the hot baking dish will keep cooking the eggs, transfer them to a serving bowl right away.

Per serving: 388 cal; 33g total fat (18g sat); 443mg chol; 659mg sodium; 4g carb; 1g fiber; 18g protein

# Cranberry Sunrise

*If you prefer, you can swap the tequila for vodka or champagne. Or, for a non-alcoholic version, go with club soda.*

Makes 8 servings (about 8 cups)
Total time: 30 minutes

**HEAT:**

| | |
|---|---|
| 2 | cups fresh *or* frozen cranberries |
| 2/3 | cup fresh orange juice |
| 1/3 | cup superfine sugar |

**COMBINE:**

| | |
|---|---|
| 6 | cups fresh orange juice |
| 2 | cups silver tequila |

**Heat** 2 cups cranberries, 2/3 cup orange juice, and sugar in a saucepan over medium to a boil, then reduce heat to low and simmer until cranberries are soft, about 5 minutes.

**Press** cranberry mixture through a fine-mesh sieve; let cool completely.

**Combine** 6 cups orange juice and tequila in a large pitcher; chill while cranberry purée cools.

**Spoon** 2 Tbsp. purée into the bottom of each of eight glasses. Slowly pour 1 cup orange-tequila mixture into each glass.

Per serving: 253 cal; 0g total fat (0g sat); 0mg chol; 3mg sodium; 31g carb; 2g fiber; 2g protein

# A Southern Spin

The best thing about this eggs and grits dish, it's good eating any time of day. Plus, poaching is a practical technique to know for cooking eggs, and not at all that hard to do. But don't worry about the vinegar in the water — you won't taste it. It's there to help the whites set up.

**GOOD TO KNOW:**
Grits

A staple in the American South, as well as northern Italy, where they're called polenta, grits are coarsely ground bits of corn. It's fine to substitute with yellow cornmeal.

# Smothered Grits & Eggs

*The creamy yolk of a poached egg is pure heaven with the smooth, hot grits. And with tomato and ham, this dish is that much better.*

Makes 4 servings (6 cups grits)
Total time: 30 minutes

**HEAT:**

| | |
|---|---|
| 4 | cups water |
| 2 | Tbsp. distilled white vinegar |

**MEANWHILE, HEAT:**

| | |
|---|---|
| 2 | cups *each* whole milk and low-sodium chicken broth |
| 1 | tsp. kosher salt |
| 1¹/₂ | cups grits *or* yellow cornmeal |
| 2 | cups frozen yellow corn kernels |
| 1 | cup diced red bell peppers |
| 1 | jalapeño, seeded and minced |
| | Salt and black pepper to taste |
| 2 | Tbsp. olive oil |
| 1 | pint grape *or* cherry tomatoes |
| 1 | cup diced cooked ham |
| ¹/₄ | cup chopped fresh cilantro |

**SLIDE:**

| | |
|---|---|
| 4 | eggs, *each* cracked into individual ramekins |
| ¹/₂ | cup crumbled feta |

To prevent lumps from forming, slowly whisk the cornmeal into the boiling milk-broth mixture.

**Heat** water and vinegar in a sauté pan to a simmer for the eggs.

**Meanwhile, heat** milk, broth, and 1 tsp. salt in a saucepan to a boil over high. Whisk in grits in a steady stream, stirring constantly; reduce heat to medium-low and cook according to package directions.

**Stir** corn, bell peppers, and jalapeño into grits; cook 3 minutes more, stirring occasionally. Season grits with salt and pepper, and reduce heat to low.

**Heat** oil in a skillet over medium-high. Add tomatoes and ham; sauté until ham begins to brown, 2 minutes. Off heat, stir in cilantro.

**Slide** eggs, one at a time, into the poaching water, then gently swirl the water to prevent sticking. Poach eggs 3–5 minutes, or to desired doneness.

**Divide** grits among four plates; top each with a poached egg, one-fourth of the tomato mixture, then sprinkle with feta.

Per serving: 617cal; 24g total fat (9g sat); 244mg chol; 883mg sodium; 71g carb; 5g fiber; 30g protein

So the tomatoes don't break down too much, sear them in oil along with the ham, just until they blister.

To keep the yolks from breaking, ease the eggs into the lightly simmering water.

# Blueberry Shrub Punch

*Shrubs were popular during America's colonial era as a cocktail or refreshing beverage and came about as a way to preserve fruit.*

Makes 4 servings
Total time: 15 minutes + marinating

**PEEL:**

| | |
|---|---|
| ¹/₂ | lemon |

**CRUSH:**

| | |
|---|---|
| 8 | oz. fresh *or* frozen blueberries, thawed if frozen |
| ³/₄ | cup sugar |
| ³/₄ | cup distilled white vinegar |

**COMBINE:**

| | |
|---|---|
| 1¹/₃ | cups vodka, chilled |
| 4 | cups club soda, chilled |
| | Crushed ice |

**Peel** lemon with a vegetable peeler. (Do not include white pith.)

**Crush** blueberries, lemon peel, and sugar in a glass bowl; let sit 30 minutes. Stir in vinegar, cover, and refrigerate at least 48 hours. Press shrub through a fine-mesh sieve; discard solids.

**Combine** shrub, vodka, and club soda with ice; serve immediately.

Per serving: 320 cal; 0g total fat (0g sat); 0mg chol; 1mg sodium; 38g carb; 0g fiber; 0g protein

# Favorite Frittata

Fluffy, cheesy eggs and crispy hash browns all in one,
does it get any better? Nope. This frittata has got it all
going on. With three cheeses, bacon, spinach, and a hash
brown crust there's not much more to say, except that
you, and your friends and family, will love this recipe.

## Spinach & Bacon Frittata
### with hash-brown crust

*Adding both heavy cream and cream cheese make for an extra-creamy frittata. And if you can't find Emmental cheese, Gruyère or Comté are OK substitutes.*

Makes 8 servings
Total time: about 1 hour

**COOK:**
| | |
|---|---|
| 8 | oz. thick-sliced bacon, diced |

**WHISK:**
| | |
|---|---|
| 6 | eggs |
| 1 | cup heavy cream |
| 4 | oz. cream cheese, softened |
| 1 | cup *each* shredded Emmental and sharp white Cheddar, divided |
| $1/2$ | cup grated Parmesan |
| $1/4$ | cup sliced scallions |
| 1 | tsp. kosher salt |
| $1/4$ | tsp. *each* cayenne pepper and black pepper |
| 3 | cups trimmed and chopped fresh spinach |

**MELT:**
| | |
|---|---|
| 1 | Tbsp. unsalted butter |
| 1 | pkg. fresh hash brown potato shreds (such as Simply Potatoes; 1 lb. 4 oz.) |

**Preheat** oven to 400°.

**Cook** bacon in a 10-inch ovenproof nonstick skillet until crisp; transfer to a paper-towel-lined plate and drain all but 1 Tbsp. drippings.

**Whisk** together eggs, cream, cream cheese, $1/2$ cup Emmental, $1/2$ cup Cheddar, Parmesan, scallions, 1 tsp. salt, cayenne, and $1/4$ tsp. black pepper; stir in spinach and bacon.

**Melt** butter with drippings in same skillet over medium-high heat. Add hash browns, spreading and pressing them up the sides; season with salt and black pepper. Reduce heat to medium; cook hash browns until edges start to brown, about 10 minutes.

**Sprinkle** remaining $1/2$ cup *each* Emmental and Cheddar over hash browns; pour egg mixture over top. Bake frittata until filling is firm and the tip of a knife inserted near the center comes out clean, 30–35 minutes. Let frittata stand 5 minutes, run a spatula around the rim, invert onto a plate, then invert again onto a serving plate.

Per serving: 571 cal; 43g total fat (22g sat); 273mg chol; 1236mg sodium; 4g carb; 2g fiber; 27g protein

## Classic Fruit Salad

*Customize this quick salad by adding any seasonal fruits of your choice.*

Makes 4 cups
Total time: 15 minutes

**HEAT:**
| | |
|---|---|
| $1/4$ | cup fresh orange juice |
| $1/3$ | cup diced dried apricots |

**POUR:**
| | |
|---|---|
| 2 | navel oranges, suprêmed |
| 1 | Granny Smith apple, diced |
| 1 | banana, sliced |
| 2 | Tbsp. chopped fresh mint |
| 1 | tsp. sugar |
| | Juice of $1/2$ a lime |
| | Pinch of salt |

**Heat** orange juice in a saucepan over medium until warm. Add apricots, remove from heat, and let stand until soft, about 10 minutes.

**Pour** juice and apricots over oranges, apple, and banana; toss with mint, sugar, lime juice, and salt. Serve salad immediately.

Per $1/2$ cup: 52 cal; 0g total fat (0g sat); 0mg chol; 0mg sodium; 14g carb; 3g fiber; 1g protein

For perfectly cooked hash browns, start them on the stove — the radiant heat will help crisp them.

To unmold, place a plate on the skillet, then flip the skillet and plate over to release the frittata.

# Fiesta Eggs

Thanks to Anaheim chiles, oregano, cumin, and paprika, this Mexican take on the classic eggs in purgatory packs a major flavor punch. Baked in a tomato sauce with black beans and finished with fresh cilantro and serrano chiles, this festive breakfast is worthy of a party.

**GOOD TO KNOW:**
Anaheim Chiles

Medium green in color with a long narrow shape, Anaheim chiles have a mild, slightly sweet taste with just a bit of a bite. Anaheims are great for stuffing or to add to salsa.

## Eggs in Tomato Sauce
### with black beans

*This savory vegetarian breakfast also makes for a great lunch or dinner. Whenever you choose to serve it, it's sure to get rave reviews.*

Makes 6 servings
Total time: 45 minutes

**HEAT:**

| | |
|---|---|
| 2 | Tbsp. olive oil |
| 2 | Anaheim chiles, seeded and diced (1 cup) |
| 1/2 | cup minced onion |
| 1 | Tbsp. minced fresh garlic |
| 1 | tsp. *each* dried oregano, ground cumin, paprika, and kosher salt |

**STIR IN:**

| | |
|---|---|
| 1 | can diced tomatoes (28 oz.), drained |
| 1 | can black beans (15 oz.), drained and rinsed |
| 1 | can tomato sauce (8 oz.) |
| 2 | tsp. hot sauce (such as Cholula) |

**CRACK:**

| | |
|---|---|
| 6 | eggs |
| 1 | cup shredded Monterey Jack cheese |
| | Fresh cilantro leaves |
| | Thinly sliced serrano chiles |

**Preheat** oven to 450°.

**Heat** oil in a 12-inch ovenproof skillet over medium. Add Anaheims and onion and cook until softened, 5 minutes. Stir in garlic, oregano, cumin, paprika, and salt; cook 1 minute.

**Stir in** diced tomatoes, beans, tomato sauce, and hot sauce. Bring sauce to a simmer; cook until it's reduced and thick, 8–10 minutes.

**Crack** eggs, add to skillet on top of sauce, and sprinkle cheese around eggs. Bake eggs until whites are cooked and yolks are still soft, 10–12 minutes (or to desired doneness). Top eggs with cilantro and serranos.

Per serving: 281 cal; 15g total fat (6g sat); 203mg chol; 1123mg sodium; 22g carb; 6g fiber; 16g protein

## Lemonade Sangría

*Cool and super refreshing, this sangría can be non-alcoholic, too. Substitute white grape juice or lemon-lime soda for the wine.*

Makes 6 servings
Total time: 10 minutes + chilling

| | |
|---|---|
| 1 | can frozen raspberry-lemonade concentrate (12 oz.), thawed in the refrigerator |
| 1 | bottle sweet white wine, 750 ml (such as Riesling *or* Gewürztraminer) |
| 1 | pkg. frozen mixed berries (12 oz.) |
| 1 | lemon, sliced |
| 2 | cups chilled club soda |

**Mix** concentrate and wine in a large pitcher. Add frozen berries and lemon slices; cover and chill until ready to serve. Just before serving, stir in club soda.

Per serving (about 1 cup): 232 cal; 0g total fat; 0mg chol; 2mg sodium; 38g carb; 2g fiber; 0g protein

To remove the raw taste of the garlic and spices, add them to the Anaheim mixture and cook briefly.

To ensure the eggs don't break, crack them into a bowl and gently add them to the skillet.

# Pizza for Breakfast

Yes, there's a place for pizza at the breakfast table. And this slightly spicy variation is sure to satisfy even the pickiest of eaters. Topped with pillowy scrambled eggs, a mix of cheeses, and a fresh pico de gallo to boot, this is one breakfast you just can't pass up.

## Breakfast Pizza
### with pico de gallo

*To bake pizza in the oven, preheat oven to 450° and bake 12 minutes.*

Makes 8 servings
Total time: 25 minutes

**FOR THE PIZZA, WHISK:**

| | |
|---|---|
| 8 | large eggs |
| 1/4 | cup milk |
| | Salt and black pepper |
| 1 | Tbsp. unsalted butter |
| 1 | cup chopped ham (4 oz.) |
| 1 | purchased pizza crust, such as Boboli (12-inch) |
| 1 | cup prepared picante sauce |
| 1 | cup shredded Cheddar and Monterey Jack cheese blend (4 oz.) |

**FOR THE PICO DE GALLO, COMBINE:**

| | |
|---|---|
| 1/3 | cup diced yellow bell pepper |
| 1/3 | cup seeded and diced tomato |
| 1/3 | cup minced scallions |

**Prepare** grill for two-zone grilling, heating one side to high and the other side to low.

**For the pizza, whisk** together eggs and milk; season with salt and pepper. Melt butter in a nonstick skillet over medium heat; add ham and sauté 3–4 minutes.

**Add** eggs and let set 1 minute. Pull eggs away from edges of skillet with a spatula, then continue to pull eggs toward center of skillet until large curds form; remove skillet from heat.

**Spread** picante sauce over crust, then top with scrambled egg mixture and cheeses. Grill pizza over low heat, covered, until crust is light brown and cheeses melt, 5–7 minutes.

**For the pico de gallo, combine** bell pepper, tomato, and scallions. To serve, remove pizza from grill and top with pico de gallo; cut into 8 slices and serve immediately.

Per serving: 283 cal; 11g total fat (6g sat); 116mg chol; 634mg sodium; 29g carb; 2g fiber; 15g protein

Sauté ham in butter, then add whisked eggs. Let eggs set 1 minute before scrambling.

Top pizza with sauce, egg mixture, and cheese, then grill until crust browns and cheese melts.

Slice bell pepper into strips, then dice. Pico de gallo can be made up to one day ahead and refrigerated.

## Tropical Fruit Salad

*Most of the fruit can be cut ahead of time, but don't slice the banana or combine fruit with the rum dressing until 5 minutes before serving.*

Makes about 4 cups
Total time: 10 minutes

| | |
|---|---|
| 1 | cup fresh mango slices |
| 1 | cup fresh pineapple chunks |
| 1 | cup hulled and halved strawberries |
| 1 | banana, sliced |
| 1/4 | cup fresh lime juice (1–2 limes) |
| 1/4 | cup sweetened shredded coconut |
| 2 | Tbsp. sugar |
| 2 | Tbsp. light rum |
| 2 | Tbsp. chopped fresh mint |

**Combine** mango, pineapple, strawberries, and banana in a large bowl.

**Whisk** together lime juice, coconut, sugar, rum, and mint; toss with fruit. Let salad stand 5 minutes before serving to macerate.

Per 1/2 cup: 73 cal; 1g total fat (1g sat); 0mg chol; 8mg sodium; 15g carb; 2g fiber; 1g protein

# Spiced Sandwich

Even the heaviest morning traffic won't phase you if you start the day with this spicy sandwich! Complete with crisp, smoky bacon, a fresh tomato and avocado salsa, and cheesy eggs atop a toasted bun, this flavor-packed sandwich will keep you going all day long.

**GOOD TO KNOW:**
Chipotle in Adobo

Chipotle chiles are dried, smoked jalapeños canned in a tangy red sauce called adobo. The chiles lend intense smoky heat to a dish, while the sauce adds a sweet-and-sour flavor.

## Chipotle Bacon Breakfast Sandwiches
### with tomato avocado salsa

*If you like a breakfast sandwich with a runny yolk, simply flip the egg and top with cheese, instead of breaking the yolk prior to flipping.*

Makes 4 sandwiches
Total time: 40 minutes

**COOK:**

| | |
|---|---|
| 8 | strips thick-sliced bacon |
| 2 | Tbsp. brown sugar |
| 1 | Tbsp. minced chipotle in adobo sauce |
| 1 | Tbsp. red wine vinegar |

**COMBINE:**

| | |
|---|---|
| 1/2 | cup quartered cherry tomatoes |
| 1/2 | cup sliced avocado, pitted |
| 2 | Tbsp. thinly sliced scallions |
| 2 | Tbsp. minced fresh cilantro |
| 1 | Tbsp. mayonnaise |
| | Juice of 1/2 a lime |
| | Salt and black pepper to taste |

**COOK:**

| | |
|---|---|
| 4 | eggs |
| 1 | Tbsp. unsalted butter |
| 4 | slices Pepper Jack cheese |
| 4 | kaiser rolls, split and toasted |

**Cook** bacon in a nonstick skillet until crisp; transfer to a paper-towel-lined plate and pour off drippings. Stir in brown sugar, chipotle, and vinegar; simmer over medium heat, 1 minute. Add bacon back to skillet to coat in glaze.

**Combine** tomatoes, avocado, scallions, cilantro, mayonnaise, and lime juice for the salsa; season with salt and pepper.

**Cook** eggs in butter over medium heat in a nonstick skillet until whites are set; season with salt and pepper. Break yolks, flip eggs, and cook 1 minute more. Top eggs with cheese, cover skillet, and let melt, 1 minute. Assemble bacon, eggs, and salsa on kaiser rolls.

Per sandwich: 596cal; 36g total fat (13g sat); 235mg chol; 1112mg sodium; 41g carb; 3g fiber; 26g protein

## Gingered Tomato Juice

*Ginger beer isn't really beer (or even alcoholic), but it is the unique flavor in this Bloody Mary spin-off. Don't mistake ginger beer for ginger ale, though — ginger ale is sweeter.*

Makes 4 drinks
Total time: 5 minutes

| | |
|---|---|
| 1 1/3 | cups vegetable-juice cocktail (such as V8) *or* tomato juice |
| 1 1/3 | cups ginger beer |
| | Worcestershire sauce and Tabasco sauce to taste |
| 4 | lemon slices |

**Fill** four tall glasses with ice, then top each with 1/3 cup vegetable-juice cocktail and 1/3 cup ginger beer; season with Worcestershire and Tabasco, then stir to blend. Garnish servings with lemon slices.

Per serving: 50 cal; 0g total fat (0g sat); 0mg chol; 56mg sodium; 13g carb; 1g fiber; 0g protein

Return the cooked bacon to the skillet and turn it in the chipotle glaze until well coated.

For ease, look for deli-sliced cheese. Then layer it over the eggs, cover skillet, and let melt for a minute.

THE EGGS
**HAVE IT!**

# Green, Eggs & Ham

Breakfast, brunch, or dinner — this riff on green eggs and ham will brighten your table no matter what time of day it appears. Made with perfectly tender asparagus, seared ham, and soft scrambled eggs, this sandwich is a healthful and satisfying delight.

## Green, Eggs & Ham Sandwiches

*If you're having difficulty finding sandwich-sized ciabatta, English muffins make a good stand-in.*

Makes 4 servings
Total time: 45 minutes

| | |
|---|---|
| 4 | Tbsp. unsalted butter, divided |
| 2 | sandwich-sized ciabatta squares, halved horizontally |
| | Salt and black pepper to taste |
| 8 | slices Canadian bacon |
| 1 | Tbsp. olive oil |
| 8 | oz. asparagus, trimmed |
| 2 | oz. goat cheese, softened |
| 1 | tsp. fresh lemon juice |
| 1/2 | tsp. minced lemon zest |
| 8 | eggs |
| 1/4 | cup half-and-half |
| | Fresh thyme leaves |

**Blanch asparagus in the same skillet. Since it's already hot, the water will boil almost instantly.**

**Preheat** oven to 400°.

**Melt** 2 Tbsp. butter, brush onto cut sides of ciabatta; season with salt and pepper. Toast bread in the oven on a baking sheet, cut side up, until golden, about 10 minutes.

**Sear** Canadian bacon in oil in a nonstick skillet over medium heat until edges curl, 1–2 minutes (3–4 minutes for thick slices). Transfer slices to a plate and tent with foil; wipe out skillet.

**Boil** 1/2 cup water in same skillet over high heat. Add asparagus and simmer until water evaporates, 3–5 minutes; transfer to a plate.

**Combine** goat cheese, lemon juice, and zest; spread onto cut sides of toasted ciabatta. Whisk together eggs and half-and-half; season with salt and pepper.

**Melt** remaining 2 Tbsp. butter in same skillet over medium heat. Add egg mixture, and scramble, stirring constantly, until nearly set. Divide eggs among each ciabatta half, top with 2 slices Canadian bacon, asparagus, and thyme. Transfer sandwiches to oven and bake 5 minutes; slice in half diagonally.

Per serving: 554 cal; 34g total fat (15g sat); 457mg chol; 1524mg sodium; 22g carb; 2g fiber; 38g protein

**Scramble the eggs until nearly set. They should be a little runny to prevent overcooking in the oven.**

**To assemble the sandwiches, first spread with goat cheese, then top with eggs, bacon, and asparagus.**

## Sidecar Punch

*Instead of more traditional breakfast cocktails, try this refreshing drink to wake you up in the morning.*

Makes 4 servings
Total time: 10 minutes

| | |
|---|---|
| 1/2 | cup brandy |
| 1/2 | cup cherry juice from maraschino cherries |
| 1/4 | cup lemonade |
| 2 | Tbsp. fresh lime juice |
| 2 | Tbsp. Triple Sec |
| | Cubed and crushed ice |
| | Lime and orange slices |
| | Maraschino cherries |

**Combine** brandy, cherry juice, lemonade, lime juice, and Triple Sec in a cocktail shaker with a few ice cubes. Shake vigorously to blend, then strain into 4 cocktail glasses filled with crushed ice.

**Garnish** each cocktail with lime, oranges, and cherries.

Per serving: 217 cal; 0g total fat (0g sat); 0mg chol; 18mg sodium; 32g carb; 0g fiber; 0g protein

# Breakfast Panini

Talk about an eye opener! These stunning breakfast sandwiches put soggy, stale fast-food fare to shame. Thick breakfast sausages and eggs cooked to your preference get piled on perfectly toasted bread then finished with and a tangy, homemade sauce.

**GOOD TO KNOW:**
Chowchow Sauce

Chowchow sauce, a mustard-flavored relish, has been enjoyed in the South for over 200 years. And although its origin is debated, no one can deny that it's a staple there.

## Breakfast Panini
### with chowchow

*Any remaining chowchow can be refrigerated for up to 2 weeks. Use as a sauce to top chicken or pork.*

Makes 4 servings (2 sandwiches)
Total time: 40 minutes

**FOR THE CHOWCHOW, SIMMER:**

| | |
|---|---|
| 1/4 | cup prepared yellow mustard |
| 2 | Tbsp. ketchup |
| 2 | Tbsp. barbecue sauce |
| 1 | Tbsp. pure maple syrup |
| 1/4 | cup minced red onion |
| 1/4 | cup sweet pickle relish |
| 1/4 | cup chopped jarred roasted red bell pepper |

**FOR THE SANDWICH, SPREAD:**

| | |
|---|---|
| 3 | Tbsp. unsalted butter, softened |
| 4 | center-cut slices of a round loaf of bread (1/2-inch thick) |

**FRY:**

| | |
|---|---|
| 12 | oz. bulk Italian sausage |

**COOK:**

| | |
|---|---|
| 4 | eggs |
| | Salt and black pepper |
| 4 | slices Cheddar cheese |

**For the chowchow, simmer** mustard, ketchup, barbecue sauce, and maple syrup in a saucepan over medium-low heat. Cook 1 minute, then stir in onion, relish, and bell pepper; set aside.

**For the sandwiches, spread** both sides of bread with butter, then toast on both sides in a large nonstick skillet over medium heat.

**Form** sausage into a 1/4-inch-thick patty. Fry sausage in skillet over medium-high heat until cooked through, 4–5 minutes per side. Remove sausage from skillet and keep warm.

**Crack** eggs into skillet with drippings; season with salt and pepper. Cook eggs over medium heat until whites are nearly set, then flip and cook until yolks start to set. Top eggs with cheese, cover skillet, and let cheese melt.

**To assemble, cut** sausage in half. Divide sausage and eggs between 2 slices of toast. Spoon chowchow over eggs, top with remaining toast slices, and cut in half.

Per half sandwich: 568 cal; 39g total fat (17g sat); 300mg chol; 1193mg sodium; 25g carb; 1g fiber; 28g protein

## Orange-ade

*Easy-dissolving superfine sugar and sparkling water add zip to fresh squeezed orange juice.*

Makes 4 drinks
Total time: 5 minutes

| | |
|---|---|
| 2 | cups fresh orange juice |
| 1/4 | cup superfine sugar |
| 2 | cups sparkling water *or* club soda |
| 4 | orange slices |

**Stir** together orange juice and sugar, then stir in sparkling water. Pour Orange-ade into ice-filled glasses; garnish with orange slices.

Per serving: 100 cal; 0g total fat (0g sat); 0mg chol; 1mg sodium; 31g carb; 1g fiber; 1g protein

Form sausage into a patty by forming into a ball, placing between sheets of plastic wrap, and pressing flat.

If you aren't keen on a runny yolk, simply break the yolks with a fork before flipping.

# Eggs & Muffins

No need to swing by the fast food joint for breakfast. With a homemade cheese sauce, thick Canadian bacon, and a fresh slice of tomato, this is a marvelous makeover of a classic. Best of all, it only takes 30 minutes, which means you're on the go in no time.

**GOOD TO KNOW:**
## Cast-Iron Skillets

All cast-iron skillets are versatile, durable, multi-purpose cooking vessels. Their biggest plus — even conduction and distribution of heat, as well as heat retention.

# Egg-Muffin Sandwiches
## with cheese sauce

*Canadian bacon is delicious on this sandwich, but keep things interesting by swapping in bacon or sausage every now and then.*

Makes 4 sandwiches
Total time: 30 minutes

**SEAR:**

| | |
|---|---|
| 4 | slices Canadian bacon |
| 2 | Tbsp. unsalted butter, divided |
| 1 | Tbsp. minced scallion whites |

**WHISK IN:**

| | |
|---|---|
| 1 | Tbsp. all-purpose flour |
| 3/4 | cup whole milk |
| 1/2 | tsp. Dijon mustard |
| 2 | oz. American cheese, diced |
| | Salt and Tabasco sauce to taste |
| 4 | eggs |
| | Black pepper to taste |
| 4 | English muffins, toasted and buttered |
| 4 | slices tomato |
| | Sliced scallion greens |

**Sear** Canadian bacon in 1 Tbsp. butter in a sauté pan over medium heat until edges curl, 1–2 minutes per side; transfer to a plate and tent with foil. Melt remaining 1 Tbsp. butter in same pan; add scallion whites and cook 1 minute.

**Whisk in** flour and cook 1 minute. Slowly whisk in milk and Dijon, whisking constantly; bring to a simmer and cook 2 minutes. Whisk in cheese until melted and smooth; season with salt and Tabasco.

**Coat** four egg rings with nonstick spray. Arrange rings in a cast-iron or nonstick skillet coated with nonstick spray and heat over medium.

**Crack** one egg into each ring. Add 2 Tbsp. water to pan (around rings). Cover skillet and steam-fry eggs until cooked through, 3–4 minutes; season with salt and pepper.

**Assemble** sandwiches by spreading a dollop of sauce on bottom half of each muffin. Top sauce with one slice Canadian bacon, one tomato slice, and one egg. Dollop egg with more sauce, garnish with scallion greens, then top with other muffin half.

Per sandwich: 437 cal; 25g total fat (13g sat); 245mg chol; 875mg sodium; 31g carb; 1g fiber; 22g protein

# Peach-Raspberry Smoothies

*Give this refreshing smoothie a try, then use the ratios to make it your own by swapping in different fruits and juices.*

Makes 4 servings (4 cups)
Total time: 5 minutes

| | |
|---|---|
| 2 1/2 | cups sliced fresh peaches, partially frozen, *or* frozen peaches, partially thawed |
| 2/3 | cup apple juice |
| 2/3 | cup vanilla yogurt |
| 1/2 | cup fresh raspberries, partially frozen, *or* frozen raspberries, partially thawed |
| 2 | cups ice chips |

**Blend** peaches, apple juice, yogurt, raspberry, and ice in a blender until smooth.

Per serving: 79 cal; 00g total fat (0g sat); 3mg chol; 28mg sodium; 18g carb; 1g fiber; 2g protein

Searing the Canadian bacon in a hot sauté pan adds flavor and texture to the breakfast sandwich.

Just 2 Tbsp. of water is all you need to add to the hot skillet to "steam-fry" the eggs.

# BREAKFAST
# CASSEROLES

This variety
of all-in-one
breakfast
dishes makes
cooking for a
crowd easy
and delicious!

# Breakfast Strudel

Here is a strudel with style and this no-fail dish is sure to bring rave reviews once it appears on your breakfast table. Besides having uptown looks and loads of flavor, it's a dream to prepare. And a three-ingredient side dish offers elevation to the meal while keeping it quick to prepare.

**GOOD TO KNOW:**
## Puff Pastry

Puff pastry is a French delicacy made by rolling cold butter into layers of dough. When baked, the butter melts and steams, causing the dough to puff. Find it in the freezer aisle.

## Breakfast Strudel

Makes 8 servings (2 strudels)
Total time: about 1 hour

| | |
|---|---|
| 1 | cup purchased frozen cubed hash brown potatoes |
| 2 | Tbsp. unsalted butter |
| 1 | cup diced red bell pepper |
| 1/2 | cup diced onion |
| 1 | cup diced smoked ham |
| 12 | eggs, divided |
| 2 | Tbsp. minced fresh chives |
| | Salt and black pepper |
| 4 | oz. cream cheese, softened |
| 2 | Tbsp. orange juice |
| 1 | box frozen puff pastry, thawed (17.3 oz.) |
| 1 | Tbsp. water |
| 2 | Tbsp. shredded Parmesan |

**Preheat** oven to 400°.

**Sauté** potatoes in butter in a large nonstick skillet over medium-high heat, 5 minutes. Add bell pepper and onion and sauté 3 minutes. Stir in ham.

**Whisk** together 11 eggs and chives, add to skillet, and scramble, stirring constantly, until nearly set; season with salt and black pepper. Off heat, stir in cream cheese and orange juice until blended; chill while working with puff pastry.

**Unfold** 1 pastry sheet on a lightly floured surface; roll to a 10×12-inch rectangle. Transfer pastry to a baking sheet-sized piece of parchment paper. Trim pastry, fill with half the egg mixture, and braid as shown in the photos, *right*. Repeat process with remaining pastry and egg filling. Transfer strudels on parchment onto two baking sheets.

**Combine** 1 egg and water; brush over tops of strudels.

**Sprinkle** strudels with Parmesan and bake until golden, 20–30 minutes; cool 5 minutes.

Per serving: 487 cal; 33g total fat (12g sat); 312mg chol; 674mg sodium; 27g carb; 2g fiber; 19g protein

Cut off the top corners of the pastry and notch the bottom to create end flaps to tuck over the filling.

Spoon half the egg mixture down the center of the pastry. Cut strips on both sides at a 45-degree angle.

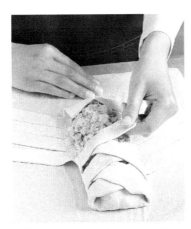

Fold up the flaps at both ends, then braid the strips across the filling and brush with egg wash.

## Broiled Grapefruit

*Choose grapefruit that are firm and brightly colored outside. Juicier ones will feel heavy for their size.*

Makes 8 servings (8 halves)
Total time: 10 minutes

| | |
|---|---|
| 4 | ruby red grapefruit, halved |
| 8 | Tbsp. brown sugar |
| 8 | tsp. sweetened shredded coconut |

**Preheat** broiler to high with rack 6 inches from element.

**Top** each grapefruit half with 1 Tbsp. brown sugar and 1 tsp. coconut; place on prepared baking sheet.

**Broil** grapefruit until coconut is toasted, 3 minutes. Watch carefully to prevent coconut from burning.

Per serving: 108 cal; 1g total fat (1g sat); 0mg chol; 5mg sodium; 26g carb; 2g fiber; 1g protein

# Breakfast Classic

Eggs Benedict is delicious, but with all its components it can feel like you need five hands to make it. This casserole version gives you the same great flavors without all the fuss. Then while the main attraction bakes, whip up a homemade hollandaise sauce to round out the meal.

# Eggs Benedict Breakfast Bread Pudding
## with spinach & parmesan

*This hearty bread pudding will please even the pickiest of breakfast traditionalists — just don't forget the hollandaise.*

Makes 12 servings
Total time: 2¹/₂ hours + chilling

**BRUSH:**

| | |
|---|---|
| 6 | Tbsp. unsalted butter, melted |
| 12 | presliced English muffins |
| | Salt and black pepper |

**SWEAT:**

| | |
|---|---|
| 2 | cups diced onions |
| 2 | Tbsp. minced fresh garlic |
| ¹/₂ | tsp. freshly grated nutmeg |
| 2 | Tbsp. olive oil |
| 1 | pkg. frozen, chopped spinach (10 oz.), thawed and squeezed dry |

**WHISK:**

| | |
|---|---|
| 4 | cups half-and-half |
| 10 | eggs |
| 1 | cup grated Parmesan |
| 3 | Tbsp. Dijon mustard |
| 1¹/₂ | tsp. kosher salt |
| ¹/₂ | tsp. cayenne pepper |

**ADD:**

| | |
|---|---|
| 12 | oz. cooked ham, torn into bite-sized pieces |

**Preheat** oven to 350°. Coat a 9×13-inch baking dish with nonstick spray.

**Brush** butter on cut sides of muffins; season with salt and black pepper. Cut muffin halves into 9 pieces each; arrange on two baking sheets.

**Toast** muffin pieces until deep golden, about 30 minutes, rotating baking sheets halfway through.

**Sweat** onions, garlic, and nutmeg in oil in a skillet over medium heat, covered, until onions soften, 5–6 minutes. Stir in spinach; cook 1 minute.

**Whisk** together half-and-half, eggs, Parmesan, Dijon, 1¹/₂ tsp. salt, and cayenne in a large bowl.

**Add** ham, toasted muffin pieces, and spinach mixture and toss to coat. Transfer mixture to prepared dish and cover with plastic wrap, pressing down so muffins begin to absorb liquid. Refrigerate pudding 3 hours or up to 1 day.

**Preheat** oven to 350°. Remove plastic wrap and cover bread pudding with foil.

**Bake** bread pudding 30 minutes. Remove foil, bake bread pudding 45 minutes more, then transfer to a rack, and let cool 15 minutes.

**Prepare** hollandaise, *right,* while bread pudding bakes. Drizzle hollandaise over each serving.

Per serving with hollandaise: 621 cal; 43g total fat (24g sat); 309mg chol; 1112mg sodium; 33g carb; 2g fiber; 24g protein

Brush split English muffins with melted butter to add more flavor and to help them brown.

Cover pudding with foil to help it bake through without browning too much on top.

# Hollandaise Sauce

Makes 1²/₃ cups
Total time: 30 minutes

**MELT:**

| | |
|---|---|
| 2 | sticks unsalted butter (16 Tbsp.) |

**REDUCE:**

| | |
|---|---|
| ¹/₃ | cup white wine vinegar |
| ¹/₃ | cup dry white wine |
| 2 | Tbsp. minced shallots |
| 1 | tsp. black peppercorns |

**WHISK:**

| | |
|---|---|
| 3 | egg yolks |
| 4 | tsp. fresh lemon juice, divided |
| | Salt and cayenne pepper to taste |

**Melt** butter in a saucepan over low heat; skim off and discard foam.

**Reduce** vinegar and wine with shallots and peppercorns in a saucepan over medium heat until it measures 3 Tbsp. strained liquid, 15–20 minutes. Simmer 1-inch water in a saucepan over medium-low heat.

**Whisk** egg yolks and vinegar reduction in a stainless steel bowl. Place bowl over simmering water (don't let bowl touch water). Whisk mixture vigorously until yolks begin to thicken and whisk begins to leave trails, 2 minutes. Remove bowl from heat.

**Off heat, whisk in** 2 tsp. lemon juice. Begin whisking butter into yolk mixture a drop at a time. As the mixture starts to thicken, whisk in remaining butter in a thin stream. If the mixture gets cold, return bowl to pan of simmering water and continue whisking in butter. Whisk in remaining lemon juice; season with salt and cayenne. If sauce seems too thick, thin with a little warm water.

**To keep sauce warm, transfer** to a heatproof vessel; place in a pan of warm water set over low heat. Stir sauce often to keep smooth.

Per Tbsp.: 69 cal; 7g total fat (5g sat); 39mg chol; 2mg sodium; 0g carb; 0g fiber; 0g protein

# Omelet Nachos

Inspired by an appetizer favorite, this gooey, cheesy, and tasty take on nachos hits the spot whether you're just starting the day, hosting a sporting event, or just hanging out with friends. You'll be hard-pressed to find someone who doesn't like these nachos, and for good reason.

**GOOD TO KNOW:**
Worcestershire

Worcestershire sauce was first bottled in Worcester, England (although it was developed in India). It's made with a plethora of flavorings and is an essential ingredient in Bloody Marys.

## Denver Omelet Nachos
### with hash-brown potatoes

*Denver omelets are just the ticket when you're hungry, but these nachos are so much more festive than an omelet.*

Makes 6–8 servings
Total time: 45 minutes

**PREPARE:**

| | |
|---|---|
| 1 | bag frozen Ore-Ida Crispy Crowns (30 oz.) |
| | Salt and black pepper |

**WHISK:**

| | |
|---|---|
| 1 | cup mayonnaise |
| 3 | Tbsp. hot sauce (such as Cholula) |
| 1/2 | tsp. grated fresh garlic |

**COOK:**

| | |
|---|---|
| 8 | oz. ham steak, diced |
| 2 | Tbsp. olive oil |
| 4 | oz. button mushrooms, diced |
| 1/2 | cup *each* diced red and green bell pepper |
| 1/2 | cup diced onion |

**WHISK:**

| | |
|---|---|
| 4 | eggs |
| 1/4 | cup whole milk |
| 1 | Tbsp. unsalted butter |

**ASSEMBLE:**

| | |
|---|---|
| 3 | cups shredded Colby Jack cheese |
| | Sliced scallion greens |

**Preheat** oven to 425°.

**Prepare** Crispy Crowns according to package directions, then season with salt and pepper.

**Whisk** together mayonnaise, hot sauce, and garlic; transfer to a squeeze bottle.

**Cook** ham in oil in a sauté pan over high heat until beginning to brown, 3–4 minutes; transfer to a paper-towel-lined plate.

**Add** mushrooms, bell pepper, and onion to pan; cook until fork-tender and moisture evaporates, 5 minutes. Transfer mushroom mixture to a bowl; stir in ham, and season with salt and pepper.

**Whisk** together eggs and milk; season with salt and pepper. Melt butter in a nonstick skillet over medium until foamy. Add eggs and scramble, stirring constantly, until nearly set; transfer to a bowl.

**Assemble** nachos by placing half the Crispy Crowns on an ovenproof baking dish; top with one third hot sauce mayonnaise and half of each the ham mixture, eggs, and cheese. Bake nachos until cheese melts, 3 minutes, then top with remaining Crispy Crowns, one third mayonnaise, and remaining ham mixture, eggs, and cheese. Bake nachos until remaining cheese melts and is bubbly, 3 minutes; top with remaining mayonnaise and scallions.

Per serving: 697 cal; 56g total fat (16g sat); 158mg chol; 1582mg sodium; 31g carb; 3g fiber; 21g protein

To prevent the eggs from becoming rubbery in the oven, slightly undercook the eggs in the skillet.

So the hot sauce mayonnaise gets evenly distributed over the Crowns, use a squeeze bottle to put it on.

## Bloody Marias

*Make the bloody Maria mix up to three days in advance, then line rims of glasses when ready to serve.*

Makes 6 servings (4 cups)
Total time: 15 minutes

**COMBINE:**

| | |
|---|---|
| 2 | Tbsp. kosher salt |
| 1/2 | tsp. ground cumin |
| | Lime wedge |

**STIR:**

| | |
|---|---|
| 3 | cups tomato juice |
| 3/4 | cup silver tequila |
| 1/4 | cup fresh lime juice |
| 2 | tsp. minced chipotle in adobo sauce |
| 2 | tsp. Worcestershire sauce |
| 2 | tsp. chopped fresh cilantro |
| 2 | tsp. grated onion |
| 1 | tsp. hot sauce (such as Tabasco) |
| | Celery salt and black pepper to taste |
| | Whole scallions |

**Combine** salt and cumin on a plate. Rub rims of 6 glasses with lime wedge, then dip into cumin salt; set glasses aside.

**Stir** together tomato juice, tequila, lime juice, chipotle, Worcestershire, cilantro, onion, and hot sauce in a pitcher. Fill prepared glasses with ice and top with Bloody Maria mixture; garnish with scallions.

Per serving: 98 cal; 0g total fat (0g sat); 0mg chol; 1014mg sodium; 6g carb; 1g fiber; 1g protein

# Chilaquiles

In Mexico, chilaquiles [chee-lah-KEE-lehs] are often eaten for breakfast as a way to use up leftovers from the previous night's meal. This menu is a streamlined way to achieve the same great flavors in a simple-to-prepare casserole that comes together quickly.

**GOOD TO KNOW:**
Chorizo

Mexican chorizo is made from fresh pork that's ground, then highly seasoned with smoked paprika, fresh garlic, chili powder, and various other spices and seasonings.

## Chorizo Chilaquiles
### with radishes & cilantro

*This Mexican breakfast favorite is simple as can be and tastes like tthe best nachos you've ever eaten in your life.*

Makes 8 servings
Total time: 45 minutes

**PULSE:**

| | |
|---|---|
| 8 | oz. ground pork |
| 2 | Tbsp. olive oil |
| 1 | Tbsp. smoked paprika |
| 1 | tsp. *each* granulated garlic and dried oregano |
| 1/2 | tsp. ground coriander |
| 1/4 | tsp. ground cumin |

**PURÉE:**

| | |
|---|---|
| 1 | jar purchased mild salsa (24 oz.) |
| 1 | chipotle in adobo sauce |
| 1/2 | cup low-sodium chicken broth |
| 1 | can black beans (15 oz.), drained and rinsed |
| 1/4 | cup chopped fresh cilantro |
| | Salt and black pepper to taste |

**LAYER:**

| | |
|---|---|
| 6 | oz. tortilla chips (8 cups) |
| 8 | oz. Monterey Jack cheese, shredded (2 cups) |
| 8 | oz. queso fresco, crumbled (2 cups) |
| 1/3 | cup sliced radishes |
| | Cilantro sprigs |

**Preheat** oven to 350°.

**Pulse** pork in a food processor until nearly a paste. Heat oil in a sauté pan over medium; add pork, paprika, garlic, oregano, coriander, and cumin. Crush chorizo with a potato masher until cooked through, 3–5 minutes.

**Purée** salsa, chipotle, and broth in food processor; add to chorizo and simmer until thick, 15 minutes. Stir in beans and chopped cilantro; season with salt and pepper.

**Layer** one-third chips in a 2-quart casserole dish; top with one-third *each* chorizo mixture and both cheeses. Repeat layering two more times. Bake chilaquiles until hot and cheese melts, 15 minutes.

**Top** chilaquiles with radishes and garnish with cilantro sprigs.

Per serving: 433 cal; 26g total fat (12g sat); 55mg chol; 913mg sodium; 32g carb; 4g fiber; 20g protein

## Pineapple Smoothies
### with banana & lime

*You can easily double this recipe, but be sure to blend it in two batches, as it won't likely fit in the blender.*

Makes 4 servings (4 cups)
Total time: 15 minutes

| | |
|---|---|
| 1 1/2 | cups pineapple juice |
| 3/4 | cup plain yogurt |
| 1/4 | of a peeled lime |
| 3 | cups diced fresh pineapple, frozen |
| 1 | banana, sliced and frozen |
| 1 | Tbsp. packed fresh mint |
| | Pinch of salt |

**Add** juice, yogurt, lime, pineapple, banana, mint, and salt to blender, in that order; blend until smooth, stopping blender to stir mixture if blender slows or stalls. Serve smoothies immediately.

Per serving: 167 cal; 1g total fat (1g sat); 4mg chol; 65mg sodium; 38g carb; 3g fiber; 3g protein

Crushing the pulsed pork with a potato masher will keep it from forming large pieces while cooking.

Add the puréed salsa mixture right to the pan with the chorizo — its flavor will intensify as it simmers.

# Kielbasa Bake

When you think German food, pretzels, mustard, sausage, and beer probably come to mind, but probably not what you'd expect to eat for brunch. Though with a few tweaks, these favorite flavors can turn into a savory meal that's just right for breakfast, brunch, or anytime of day.

## Kielbasa & Pretzel Breakfast Bake

*Can't wait for the pretzel bread to stale? Place the cubed bread on a baking sheet, pop it into a 200° oven for about 1 hour, then cool.*

Makes 8 servings
Total time: 1½ hours + staling and soaking overnight

**STALE:**
| | |
|---|---|
| 1 | lb. pretzel bread, cubed |

**BROWN:**
| | |
|---|---|
| 1 | pkg. kielbasa, halved lengthwise and sliced (14 oz.) |
| 1 | Tbsp. canola oil |
| 2 | cups sliced onions |
| 1 | Tbsp. minced fresh garlic |

**WHISK:**
| | |
|---|---|
| 10 | eggs |
| 1½ | cups heavy cream |
| ½ | cup low-sodium beef broth |
| ½ | cup spicy brown mustard |
| 2 | Tbsp. chopped fresh chives |
| 2 | tsp. chopped fresh thyme |
| 2 | tsp. kosher salt |
| 1 | tsp. black pepper |
| 8 | oz. shredded Gruyère, divided |

**Stale** bread on a baking sheet until completely dry.

**Preheat** oven to 375°. Coat a 9×13-inch baking dish with nonstick spray.

**Brown** kielbasa in oil in a large skillet over high heat, 3–5 minutes; transfer to a paper-towel-lined plate and reserve drippings. Reduce heat to medium. Add onions and garlic to drippings and cook 1–2 minutes; transfer to a bowl.

**Whisk** together eggs, cream, broth, mustard, chives, thyme, salt, and pepper in a large bowl. Add bread; toss to coat. Add kielbasa, onion mixture, and half the Gruyère; transfer to prepared baking dish, cover with plastic wrap, and let sit in the refrigerator overnight.

**Sprinkle** remaining half of Gruyère over casserole; bake until a thermometer inserted into center registers 160°, about 45 minutes. Let casserole rest 15 minutes before serving.

Per serving: 675 cal; 45g total fat (22g sat); 370mg chol; 1402mg sodium; 38g carb; 2g fiber; 30g protein

## Black Forest Hot Chocolate

Makes 12 servings (3 cups)
Total time: 20 minutes

| | |
|---|---|
| 1 | cup cherry liqueur |
| 1 | cup heavy cream |
| 1 | cup whole milk |
| ½ | cup sugar |
| 4 | oz. bittersweet bar chocolate, finely chopped |
| 4 | oz. semisweet bar chocolate, finely chopped |
| | Whipped cream |

**Reduce** cherry liqueur in a saucepan over medium-high heat until syrupy, 10–12 minutes.

**Whisk in** cream until cherry mixture dissolves, then whisk in milk and sugar; bring to a simmer.

**Combine** chocolate in a bowl; pour cream mixture over the top, cover, let sit 5 minutes, then whisk until smooth. Top hot chocolate with whipped cream.

Per serving: 217 cal; 16g total fat (9g sat); 29mg chol; 17mg sodium; 19g carb; 1g fiber; 2g protein

An easy way to dry out the cubed bread is to let it sit uncovered on a baking sheet overnight.

Toss dried cubes with egg mixture to fully coat them, and so they start absorbing liquid immediately.

# Hash Brown Casserole

Whether it's for breakfast, brunch, or the last game of the season, this classic party mainstay is sure to make you the most popular host on the block. And with the addition of creamy chive-sour cream dip and crisp smoky bacon, this casserole is that much better.

**GOOD TO KNOW:**
Corn Flakes

When the Kellogg brothers accidentally flaked wheat berry they continued experimenting until they flaked corn. In 1906 the first batch of Kellogg's Corn Flakes was launched.

## Bacon-Scallion Hash Brown Casserole

*Chive-flavored sour cream dip was preferred in the Test Kitchen, but any savory option will work here, so feel free to choose your favorite flavor.*

Makes 12 servings
Total time: 1¼ hours

**COOK:**

| | |
|---|---|
| 1 | lb. thick-sliced bacon, diced |
| ¼ | cup sliced scallion whites |

**WHISK IN:**

| | |
|---|---|
| 2 | pkg. purchased chive-sour cream dip (8 oz. *each*) |
| 2 | cups shredded mild Cheddar |
| 1 | cup whole milk |
| 1 | cup sliced scallion greens |
| 4 | oz. cream cheese, softened |
| 1 | bag frozen hash browns (30 oz.), thawed |
| | Salt and black pepper to taste |

**COMBINE:**

| | |
|---|---|
| 4 | cups corn flakes cereal, crushed |
| 4 | Tbsp. unsalted butter, melted |

**Preheat** oven to 350°. Coat a 9×13-inch baking dish with nonstick spray.

**Cook** bacon in a sauté pan until crisp; transfer to a paper-towel-lined plate. Drain all but 1 Tbsp. drippings from pan. Add scallion whites and sweat over medium heat until softened, about 1 minute; transfer to a large bowl.

**Whisk in** dip, Cheddar, milk, scallion greens, and cream cheese. Stir in hash browns and bacon, season with salt and pepper, then transfer to prepared baking dish.

**Combine** corn flakes and butter, season with salt and pepper, and sprinkle over casserole.

**Bake** casserole until golden and bubbly, about 45 minutes.

Per serving: 497 cal; 34g total fat (14g sat); 80mg chol; 1300mg sodium; 26g carb; 2g fiber; 21g protein

## Mint Julep Fruit Salad

*For the best flavor, allow the tossed salad to sit in the mint julep syrup at least 1 hour before serving.*

Makes 12 servings (about 8 cups)
Total time: 15 minutes + chilling

| | |
|---|---|
| 1 | cup water |
| ½ | cup sugar |
| | Pinch of salt |
| 1 | Tbsp. bourbon |
| 4 | cups cubed fresh pineapple |
| 2 | cups cubed watermelon |
| 2 | cups cubed honeydew melon |
| 2 | Tbsp. minced fresh mint |

**Bring** water, sugar, and salt to a boil in a saucepan.

**Reduce** heat to medium and simmer 5 minutes. Cool syrup in pan set inside a bowl of ice water until cold; stir in bourbon.

**Combine** pineapple, watermelon and honeydew in a bowl, toss with syrup. Chill salad, covered, 1 hour or overnight, stirring occasionally.

**Stir in** mint just before serving.

Per serving: 68 cal; 0g total fat (0g sat); 0mg chol; 6mg sodium; 18g carb; 1g fiber; 1g protein

To ensure the bacon remains crisp as it bakes in the casserole, it must be well done before adding it in.

So the casserole holds together nicely, be sure to choose shredded hash browns as opposed to diced.

# QUINTESSENTIAL
## QUICHE

# Asparagus & Mushroom Quiche
## with arugula and prosciutto

*Quiche is special occasion breakfast or brunch fare, and this recipe epitomizes celebration.*
*Check out two additional filling options on pages 84 and 85 for quiches everyone will love.*

Makes 8 servings; Total time: 2¹/₂–3 hours + chilling & resting

**FOR THE CRUST, COMBINE:**

| | |
|---|---|
| 2 | cups all-purpose flour, divided |
| 1 | tsp. kosher salt |
| 1¹/₂ | sticks cold unsalted butter (12 Tbsp.), cubed |
| 4 | oz. cold cream cheese, cubed |
| 3–4 | Tbsp. ice water |

**FOR THE CUSTARD, WHISK:**

| | |
|---|---|
| 8 | eggs |
| 2 | cups half-and-half |
| 1¹/₂ | tsp. kosher salt |
| ¹/₂ | tsp. white pepper |
| | Pinch of freshly grated nutmeg |
| | Black pepper |

**FOR THE FILLING, MELT:**

| | |
|---|---|
| 2 | Tbsp. unsalted butter, divided |
| 8 | oz. cremini mushrooms, trimmed and sliced |
| ¹/₂ | bunch asparagus (8 oz.), trimmed, and cut into 1-inch pieces |
| 1 | bunch scallions, whites minced, greens sliced |
| 3 | oz. prosciutto, diced |
| 1 | cup shredded Gruyère cheese |
| 2 | cups arugula |

**For the crust, combine** 1 cup flour and salt in the bowl of a stand mixer fitted with the paddle attachment. Add butter and cream cheese; blend on medium-low speed until fully incorporated.

**Add** remaining 1 cup flour and 3 Tbsp. ice water; mix to combine. (Add remaining 1 Tbsp. water if dough doesn't come together.) Shape dough into a disk, cover with plastic wrap, and chill at least 1 hour or overnight.

**Preheat** oven to 375° with a baking stone set on middle rack.

**Roll** dough on a lightly floured surface into an 11–12-inch circle, ¹/₄-inch thick; roll around edges to create a thin 1-inch border. Transfer dough to a 9-inch deep-dish pie plate and gently press into bottom and up sides. Fold edges under and crimp. Freeze crust 20 minutes, then line with parchment paper and fill with dried beans.

**Bake** crust until edges are golden and bottom is set, 40–45 minutes. Remove parchment and beans, and bake crust until bottom is golden brown, 15–20 minutes more.

**For the custard, whisk** together eggs, half-and-half, salt, white pepper, and nutmeg.

**Reduce** oven heat to 325°.

**For the filling, melt** 1 Tbsp. butter in a skillet over high heat until foamy; add mushrooms and sauté until browned, 8–10 minutes. Add asparagus and scallion whites and cook 2 minutes; season with salt and black pepper, then transfer to a bowl to cool. Melt remaining 1 Tbsp. butter in same skillet over medium-high heat. Add prosciutto and cook until crisp, about 5 minutes; transfer to a paper-towel-lined plate.

**Combine** mushroom mixture, scallion greens, prosciutto, Gruyère, and arugula; arrange in hot crust, and pour custard over the top.

**Bake** quiche until edges are set and center is slightly jiggly, 1¹/₂–2 hours; (if crust starts to get too brown, cover with foil). Cool quiche at least 2 hours before serving.

Per serving: 574 cal; 42g total fat (24g sat); 300mg chol; 1079mg sodium; 30g carb; 2g fiber; 21g protein

To accommodate for crimping, roll perimeter of dough thinner while maintaining thickness of the rest.

So the crust doesn't puff up, fill the crust with dried beans until the bottom of the crust is set.

To ensure a leak-free quiche, add the filling and custard while the crust is still hot from the oven.

## Double Cheddar & Broccoli Quiche

*Cheddar and broccoli are a classic pairing and they're proving it again in this quiche.*

Makes 8 servings
Total time: 2¹/₂ hours + chilling & resting

**PREPARE:**
1      recipe Crust, *page 83*
**PREPARE:**
1      recipe Custard, *page 83*

**FOR THE FILLING, MELT:**
1      Tbsp. unsalted butter
1      cup diced yellow onions
1      cup shredded sharp Cheddar
1      cup shredded mild Cheddar
2      cups small broccoli florets

**Prepare and bake** crust according to recipe directions on page 83.
**Prepare** custard according to recipe directions on page 83.
**Reduce** oven heat to 325°.
**For the filling, melt** butter in a skillet over medium heat until foamy; add onions and cook until softened and translucent, 5 minutes. Let onions cool, then combine with sharp and mild Cheddar, and broccoli; arrange in hot crust and pour custard over the top.
**Bake** quiche until edges are set and center is slightly jiggly, about 1¹/₂ hours; (if crust starts to get too brown, cover with foil). Cool quiche at least 2 hours before serving.

Per serving: 587 cal; 44g total fat (25g sat); 303mg chol; 934mg sodium; 29g carb; 1g fiber; 20g protein

## Italian Sausage Quiche
### with roasted red peppers

Makes 8 servings
Total time: 2¹/₂ hours + chilling & resting

**PREPARE:**
1    recipe Crust, *page 83*

**PREPARE:**
1    recipe Custard, *page 83*

**FOR THE FILLING, SAUTÉ:**
6    oz. bulk Italian sausage
¹/₂    cup diced yellow onion
¹/₂    tsp. minced fresh garlic
1    Tbsp. olive oil
1    cup shredded fontina cheese
¹/₂    cup shredded Parmesan
¹/₂    cup chopped jarred roasted red peppers, patted dry
2    Tbsp. chopped fresh parsley
1    tsp. dried Italian seasoning
¹/₂    tsp. fennel seeds, chopped
¹/₂    tsp. red pepper flakes

**Prepare and bake** crust according to recipe directions on page 83.
**Prepare** custard according to recipe directions on page 83.
**Reduce** oven heat to 325°.
**For the filling, sauté** sausage, onion, and garlic in oil in a skillet over medium heat until sausage is cooked through, about 5 minutes. Transfer sausage mixture to a paper-towel-lined plate, then press dry with additional paper towels.
**Toss** sausage mixture with fontina, Parmesan, roasted peppers, parsley, Italian seasoning, fennel seeds, and pepper flakes; arrange in hot crust. Pour custard over the top.
**Bake** quiche until edges are set and center is slightly jiggly, about 1¹/₂ hours; (if crust starts to get too brown, cover with foil).

**Cool** quiche at least 2 hours before serving.

Per serving: 616 cal; 47g total fat (25g sat); 304mg chol; 1168mg sodium; 29g carb; 1g fiber; 22g protein

To cut down on grease, firmly press the cooked Italian sausage between paper towels until dry.

# COOKING WITH
# OATS

Think outside of
your daily bowl
of oatmeal and
try one of these
unique culinary
creations.

# Granola Bars

If you're a fan of granola bars, you're in for a treat. Not only are these bars sweet, nutty, and dipped in chocolate, but they're also packed with heart-healthy ingredients like cashews, currants, flax seeds, and chia seeds.

## Chocolate-Dipped Granola Bars
### with cashews & currants

Makes 8 bars
Total time: about 1 hour

**TOAST:**
2¹/2 cups old-fashioned rolled oats
1¹/2 cups whole raw cashews, divided
3 Tbsp. canola oil
2 Tbsp. flax seeds

**HEAT:**
¹/2 cup honey
¹/2 cup packed light brown sugar
³/4 tsp. table salt
¹/2 tsp. ground cinnamon

**TOSS:**
¹/2 cup dried currants
2 Tbsp. chia seeds

**MELT:**
4 oz. semisweet bar chocolate, finely chopped

**Preheat** oven to 350°. Coat an 8×8-inch pan with nonstick spray.

**Toast** oats and cashews on separate baking sheets until golden, 20 minutes.

**Purée** 1 cup cashews with oil in a mini food processor until smooth. Grind flax seeds in a spice grinder until fine.

**Heat** honey, brown sugar, salt, and cinnamon in a saucepan over medium until sugar dissolves, 3–4 minutes. Off heat, stir in puréed cashews and ground flax.

**Toss** together toasted oats, remaining ¹/2 cup cashews, currants, and chia seeds; stir in honey mixture until combined.

**Press** oat mixture into prepared pan using the back of a spatula coated with nonstick spray.

**Bake** bars 10 minutes; let cool, then cut into eight bars.

**Melt** chocolate in a microwave in 20 second intervals, stirring each time, until melted. Dip bottoms of granola bars in chocolate, letting excess drip off; place on parchment paper and allow to set up.

Per bar: 540 cal; 26g total fat (7g sat); 0mg chol; 226mg sodium; 72g carb; 5g fiber; 9g protein

# Spiced Oatmeal

Who doesn't want to start the day off right? A slow cooker makes it easy to have hot steel-cut oatmeal ready when you wake up. Just set up the slow cooker before you hit the hay, and a comforting breakfast will be waiting for you in the morning.

### Chai-Spiced Steel-Cut Oatmeal
#### with bananas & almonds

*A bowl of oatmeal is a hearty and satisfying way to start your day. Top servings with sliced bananas and crunchy almonds for a treat.*

Makes 6 servings (4¹/₂ cups)
Prep time: 10 minutes
Cook time: 7–8 hours (low)

**COMBINE:**

| | |
|---|---|
| 2 | cups water |
| 1 | cup half-and-half |
| 1 | cup steel-cut oats |
| 1 | banana, mashed |
| ¹/₂ | cup honey |
| 1¹/₂ | tsp. kosher salt |
| ¹/₂ | tsp. freshly grated nutmeg |
| ¹/₄ | tsp. *each* ground cardamom, cinnamon, and black pepper |
| ¹/₈ | tsp. *each* ground cloves and ginger |
| 1 | Lady Grey tea bag |

**STIR IN:**

| | |
|---|---|
| 1 | tsp. vanilla bean paste *or* extract |
| | Toasted sliced almonds |
| | Sliced bananas |

**Combine** water, half-and-half, oats, mashed banana, honey, salt, nutmeg, cardamom, cinnamon, pepper, cloves, and ginger in a 4-cup Pyrex measuring cup; add tea bag, pressing into liquid.

**Place** measuring cup inside a 6- to 8-qt. slow cooker. Add water to slow cooker to come halfway up the side of the measuring cup. Cover slow cooker and cook oats until al dente on low setting, 7–8 hours. Discard tea bag.

**Stir in** vanilla and top servings with almonds and bananas.

Per serving: 212 cal; 6g total fat (3g sat); 15mg chol; 500mg sodium; 38g carb; 2g fiber; 3g protein

**The slow cooker acts as a hot water bath to cook the oats gently so they don't scorch or overcook.**

# Southwest Oat Cakes

Packed with bacon, cheese, and spices, these oatmeal cakes are an all-in-one breakfast. And topped with avocado slices, salsa, and sour cream, these cakes take you straight to the tasty Southwest.

## Southwestern Oatmeal Cakes
### with bacon & cheddar

Makes 8 cakes
Total time: about 1 hour + chilling

**COOK:**

| | |
|---|---|
| 4 | strips thick-sliced bacon, diced |
| 8 | scallions, sliced (whites and greens separated) |
| 1 1/2 | tsp. *each* ground cumin, coriander, and granulated garlic |
| 1/2 | tsp. kosher salt |

**STIR IN:**

| | |
|---|---|
| 2 | cups old-fashioned rolled oats |
| 1 1/4 | cups low-sodium chicken broth |
| 1 1/4 | cups water |

**STIR IN:**

| | |
|---|---|
| 6 | oz. sharp white Cheddar, shredded (2 1/4 cups) |
| 3 | Tbsp. chopped pickled jalapeños |
| 1/3 | cup old-fashioned rolled oats, ground until fine |

**HEAT:**

| | |
|---|---|
| 6 | Tbsp. olive oil |
| | Purchased salsa, sliced avocado, and sour cream |

**Coat** an 8 1/4×4 1/4-inch loaf pan with nonstick spray.

**Cook** bacon in a saucepan until crisp; transfer to a paper-towel-lined plate. Discard all but 2 Tbsp. drippings. Sweat scallion whites with cumin, coriander, garlic, and salt in drippings over medium-low heat until scallions soften, 3 minutes. Increase heat to high.

**Stir in** 2 cups oats to coat with drippings, then add broth and water; Bring to a boil. Reduce heat to medium, and simmer until liquid is absorbed and oatmeal is very thick, stirring frequently, 6–7 minutes; transfer to a bowl and allow steam to subside.

**Stir in** Cheddar, jalapeños, bacon, and scallion greens. Transfer oatmeal to prepared pan, pressing down; cover with plastic wrap and chill until firm, 5 hours, or overnight.

**Preheat** oven to 350° with a baking sheet inside.

**Invert** oatmeal loaf onto a cutting board and cut crosswise, using a serrated knife, into 8 equal slices. Coat both sides of oatmeal slices in ground oats, pressing so they adhere, tapping off excess.

**Heat** 3 Tbsp. oil in a large cast-iron skillet over high until shimmering. Fry oatmeal slices, in two batches, until golden on both sides, 8–10 minutes per batch; transfer to oven to keep warm. Wipe out skillet and repeat with remaining 3 Tbsp. oil and oatmeal slices.

**Serve** oatmeal cakes with salsa, avocado, and sour cream.

Per cake: 304 cal; 22g total fat (6g sat); 28mg chol; 519mg sodium; 19g carb; 3g fiber; 11g protein

# Oat Scones

For an extra-special start to your day, these oat scones are irresistible. Just drizzle these dandies with a sweet glaze and watch as they get devoured.

## Cinnamon Roll Oat Scones

*These scones are great on their own, but even better with a little butter.*

Makes 8 scones
Total time: 1 hour + freezing

### FOR THE DOUGH, WHISK:

| | |
|---|---|
| 2 | cups all-purpose flour |
| 1 | cup old-fashioned rolled oats |
| 1/3 | cup packed light brown sugar |
| 2 | tsp. baking powder |
| 1 | tsp. ground cinnamon |
| 1/2 | tsp. table salt |

### CUT:

| | |
|---|---|
| 1 | stick cold unsalted butter (8 Tbsp.), cubed |
| 1/2 | cup chopped pecans, toasted |
| 1 | cup heavy cream |

### FOR THE FILLING, COMBINE:

| | |
|---|---|
| 6 | Tbsp. unsalted butter, softened |
| 6 | Tbsp. packed light brown sugar |
| 1 | tsp. ground cinnamon |

### FOR THE GLAZE, WHISK:

| | |
|---|---|
| 1/2 | cup powdered sugar, sifted |
| 3 | Tbsp. heavy cream |
| 1/2 | tsp. pure vanilla extract |

**Preheat** oven to 425°.

**For the dough, whisk** together flour, oats, brown sugar, baking powder, cinnamon, and salt.

**Cut** butter into flour mixture using a pastry blender until the pieces are pea-sized; stir in pecans. Add cream to dough mixture; stir until combined. Turn dough onto a floured piece of parchment paper; lightly sprinkle dough with additional flour. Top with a second sheet of parchment. Gently roll (or pat) dough into a 10-inch square.

**For the filling, combine** butter, brown sugar, and cinnamon to form a paste; spread onto dough. Roll dough, jelly roll-style, into a log and cover with plastic wrap; freeze 15 minutes.

**Slice** dough log into eight scones. Place scones in jumbo muffin cups.

**Bake** scones until golden, 22–25 minutes.

**For the glaze, whisk** together powdered sugar, cream, and vanilla. When cool enough to handle, but still warm, remove scones from muffin cups and drizzle with glaze.

Per scone: 600 cal; 39g total fat (22g sat); 102mg chol; 305mg sodium; 60g carb; 3g fiber; 6g protein

# Fruity Granola

Get your morning going with a granola filled with tiny bites of sweet-tart dried cranberries, crisp coconut, citrusy orange marmalade, and a sprinkling of warm spices. It tastes divine served with creamy vanilla yogurt and fresh raspberries.

### Cranberry-Orange Granola

Makes 12 servings (about 6 cups)
Total time: 50 minutes + cooling

- 2½ cups old-fashioned rolled oats
- 1 cup chopped walnuts
- ½ cup *each* packed light brown sugar and sweet orange marmalade
- 1½ tsp. ground cinnamon
- ½ tsp. ground ginger
- ¼ tsp. freshly grated nutmeg
  Zest and juice of 1 orange
  Pinch of salt
- 1 cup *each* dried cranberries and raw coconut flakes
  Vanilla Greek yogurt and fresh raspberries

**Preheat** oven to 350°.

**Toast** oats and walnuts on two separate baking sheets until golden and fragrant, 15 minutes. Line a baking sheet with parchment paper.

**Heat** brown sugar, marmalade, cinnamon, ginger, nutmeg, zest, orange juice, and salt in a skillet over medium until sugar dissolves, 3–4 minutes.

**Toss** oats, walnuts, cranberries, and coconut flakes with brown sugar mixture until coated; arrange on prepared baking sheet in a single layer.

**Bake** granola until golden brown, 30 minutes, stirring halfway through. Press granola into clumps, if desired; let cool on baking sheet.

**Serve** granola with yogurt and raspberries; store in an airtight container.

Per serving: 245 cal; 9g total fat (2g sat); 0mg chol; 33mg sodium; 40g carb; 3g fiber; 4g protein

Adding marmalade to the mix creates a viscous syrup to coat the granola, which keeps it crisp.

# Tasty Tart

For breakfast, dessert, or a midday snack, this grapefruit tart with its cookie-like oatmeal crust and sprinkling of sea salt is definitely a treat worth savoring again and again.

## Grapefruit Tart
with oatmeal-brown sugar crust

Makes 12 servings (one 9-inch tart)
Total time: 35 minutes + cooling

**FOR THE CRUST, PULSE:**

- 1³/4 cups old-fashioned rolled oats
- ³/4 cup all-purpose flour
- ¹/2 cup packed brown sugar
- 2 Tbsp. minced grapefruit zest, divided
- 1 Tbsp. minced fresh ginger
- ¹/2 tsp. table salt
- 1 stick unsalted butter (8 Tbsp.), melted

**FOR THE FILLING, COMBINE:**

- 1 pkg. cream cheese (8 oz.), softened
- ¹/3 cup sour cream
- 2 Tbsp. brown sugar
- 3 cups fresh grapefruit segments
  Coarse sea salt

**Preheat** oven to 350°.

**For the crust, pulse** oats, flour, brown sugar, 1 Tbsp. zest, ginger, and salt in a food processor until oats are chopped. With the machine running, drizzle butter into mixture until it clumps.

**Press** crust mixture into bottom and up sides of a 9-inch square (or round) tart pan with a removable bottom. Bake crust until firm, 20 minutes. Let crust cool to room temperature.

**For the filling, combine** cream cheese, sour cream, brown sugar, and remaining 1 Tbsp. zest in a bowl with a mixer on medium speed until smooth. Spread filling over crust. Arrange grapefruit segments on top of filling.

**Sprinkle** coarse sea salt over tart.

Per serving: 277 cal; 16g total fat (9g sat); 45mg chol; 163mg sodium; 31g carb; 2g fiber; 4g protein

To ensure the crust holds together, firmly press it into the bottom and up the sides of the tart pan.

# BREAKFAST & BRUNCH
## VISUAL INDEX

**9** Cinnamon Roll Coffee Cake

**10** New York Crumb Cake

**7** Brie & Cherry Braid

**11** Mocha Coffee Cakes

**13** Cinnamon Rolls

**15** Sticky Buns

**17** Sour Cream & Chocolate Old-Fashioned Doughnuts

**21** Variety-Pack Donut Muffins

**23** Cranberry-Pecan Scones

**25** Basic Buttermilk Biscuits

**25** Apricot Pecan Butter

**29** Ricotta Pancakes

**30** Pecan Praline Pancake Syrup

**31** Peach Bellini Pancake Syrup

**31** Blueberry Agrodolce Pancake Syrup

**33** Classic Swedish Pancakes

**35** Spiced Orange Baked French Toast

**35** Homemade Breakfast Sausage Patties

**37** Swiss Eibrot

**37** Sugar & Spice Bacon

**39** Hash Brown "Omelet"

**39** Fruit Cocktail

**40** Golden Hash Browns

**41** Country-Style Hash Browns

**47** Basic Omelet

**48** Spinach-Artichoke Filling

**49** Huevos Rancheros Omelets

**51** Cheesy Scrambled Egg Bake

**51** Cranberry Sunrise

**53** Smothered Grits & Eggs

**53** Blueberry Shrub Punch

**55** Spinach & Bacon Frittata

**55** Classic Fruit Salad

**57** Eggs in Tomato Sauce

**57** Lemonade Sangría

# BREAKFAST & BRUNCH
## VISUAL INDEX

**59** Breakfast Pizza

**59** Tropical Fruit Salad

**61** Chipotle Bacon Breakfast Sandwiches

**61** Gingered Tomato Juice

**63** Green, Eggs & Ham Sandwiches

**63** Sidecar Punch

**65** Breakfast Panini

**65** Orange-ade

**67** Egg-Muffin Sandwiches

**67** Peach-Raspberry Smoothies

**71** Breakfast Strudel

**71** Broiled Grapefruit

**73** Eggs Benedict Breakfast Bread Pudding with Hollandaise Sauce

**75** Denver Omelet Nachos

**75** Bloody Marias

**77** Chorizo Chilaquiles

**77** Pineapple Smoothies

**79** Kielbasa & Pretzel Breakfast Bake

**79** Black Forest Hot Chocolate

**81** Bacon-Scallion Hash Brown Casserole

**81** Mint Julep Fruit Salad

**83** Asparagus & Mushroom Quiche

**84** Double Cheddar & Broccoli Quiche

**85** Italian Sausage Quiche

**88** Chocolate-Dipped Granola Bars

**89** Chai-Spiced Steel-Cut Oatmeal

**90** Southwestern Oatmeal Cakes

**91** Cinnamon Roll Oat Scones

**92** Cranberry-Orange Granola

**93** Grapefruit Tart

# *breakfast* & BRUNCH.

10

93

71

# RECIPE INDEX